The Ultimate Potato Book

The Ultimate

Potato Book

Hundreds of Ways
to Turn America's Favorite
Side Dish into a Meal

BRUCE WEINSTEIN &
MARK SCARBROUGH

WILLIAM MORROW
An Imprint of HarperCollins*Publishers*

HarperCollins books may be purchased for educational, business, or sales promotional use. For information please write: Special Markets Department, HarperCollins Publishers Inc., 10 East 53rd Street, New York, NY 10022.

FIRST EDITION

Designed by Mary Austin Speaker

Printed on acid-free paper

Library of Congress Cataloging-in-Publication Data

Weinstein, Bruce, 1960–
    The ultimate potato book : hundreds of ways to turn America's favorite side dish into a meal / Bruce Weinstein and Mark Scarbrough.—1st ed.
        p.   cm.
    ISBN 0-06-009675-6
    1. Cookery (Potatoes)   2. Potatoes.   I. Scarbrough, Mark.   II. Title.

TX803.P8 W43   2002
641.6'521—dc21

                                                                                    2002027629

03 04 05 06 07 WBC/QW 10 9 8 7 6 5 4 3 2 1

Contents

Acknowledgments

At HarperCollins, we'd like to thank the team that has made a success of all the Ultimate books: Harriet Bell, for once again having great vision in a world where they say single subject books don't sell; Ann Cahn, for expert editorial production; Roberto de Vicq de Cumptich, for eye-catching art direction; Carrie Weinberg and Gypsy Lovett, for spot-on publicity; Kate Stark for pitch-perfect marketing. In terms of the potato book particularly: Ginger McRae, for attention to a zillion copyediting details; as well as Mary Speaker, for eye-friendly design.

At Writer's House: Susan Ginsburg, for endless consultations (yet still honest friendship); Annie Leuenberger, for undaunted fire-fighting.

In the city: Beatriz de Costa, for crystal-clear, natural-light photographs; David Weinstein, Lisa Aiello, and Vox Design, for designing www.ultimatecook.com, and for having an apparently limitless hunger for potatoes.

Around the country: Paula Yarkoni in Fair Lawn, New Jersey, for childhood recipes and advice; and Kyoko Yagi, in Austin, Texas, for patient explanations of Asian cooking techniques.

Introduction

Here's the most radical thing we can tell you: *The Ultimate Potato Book* is a book of main courses.

That may not seem like much—until you think about potatoes. They're side dishes, right? Mashed, roasted, fried, whatever. Sometimes they make a main course debut in a soup; usually they're relegated to the edge of the plate.

We've decided to put them front and center.

The recipes are alphabetized, mostly without the word "potato" in their titles: *Lasagna,* in other words, not "Potato Lasagna." If you thumb through the book, you'll get the hang of how it works. But we'll admit it right up front: some of our cataloguing is idiosyncratic. *Provençal Stew,* for example. It's a potato/tomato stew with Pernod.

Some main courses naturally include potatoes on the side. *Steak Frites,* for example. But the potatoes aren't really a "side" so much as a co-dish, half the whole, integral to the entree.

Although we're passionate about potatoes as main courses, you may still want to make them as traditional sides. To do so, find recipes like *Steak Frites* where potatoes are half the whole and just make the potato part. Here's a list:

+ Basic Boiled Potatoes (in Borscht, page 40, or Raclette, page 170)
+ Duchess Potatoes (in Beef Stew with Duchess Potatoes, page 35)
+ French Fries (in Fish and Chips, page 75)
+ Hash Browns (in Roesti, page 181)
+ Mashed Potatoes (a sour cream version in Bangers and Mash, page 30)
+ Mashed Potatoes (a more traditional version in Shepherd's Pie, page 189)
+ Oven-Roasted Fries (in Chili Fries, page 54)

- Pan-Roasted Potatoes (in Potatoes Sarladaise, page 155)
- Potato Pancakes (in Latkes, page 114)
- Shoestring Fries (in Steak Frites, page 212)

Finally, a word about potatoes. With the astounding abundance in North American markets, there are hundreds of varieties, but not all are widely available. Yes, Bintjes might be best for, say, French fries; Yellow Finns, for a gratin. But Bintjes and Yellow Finns are simply not available everywhere.

There's no reason to be fussy. Most of us walk into the supermarket and see bins filled with "baking potatoes," "yellow-fleshed potatoes," "sweet potatoes," and other generics—or if we're lucky, "Russets," "Yukon Golds," "Garnet Yams," and two or three more varietals. Therefore, these recipes were developed with broad categories in mind, rather than specific varietals. Yes, we always make suggestions: "red-skinned potatoes, such as French Fingerlings." But these are just suggestions, helpful only if you live near some well-stocked gourmet store or farmer's market.

True enough, a Russian Banana might be better than a Yukon Gold for Fondue. But unwarranted snobbishness does not get dinner on the table.

A Potato Primer

A Short History of the Spud:
From Deadly Poison to Culinary Staple

According to some, the Irish, with their monasteries and books, saved Western civilization after the fall of Rome. And to cure the famines that ravaged the Emerald Isle, farmers planted potatoes, which saved the Irish. So by that logic, the lowly spud saved. . . . Well, we wouldn't want to overstate the case, would we?

Truth be told, the potato was once feared in the West as a fiend, something straight out of the ground, like the devil. What nefarious activity was it carrying on down there?

But long before Europeans were superstitious about the potato, it was cultivated in the high Andes, having been brought up from the Chilean coast sometime in the fourth millennium B.C. Modern blue potatoes, by the by, are the closest cousins of these original potatoes. Simply put, the spud survived in high altitudes and at frigid temperatures where corn didn't.

From there, the history of the potato gets mixed up with that other, older history of the strong subjugating the weak. The Incas conquered the tribes around Lake Titicaca, in the Peru-Bolivia region, and so the potato spread throughout their empire. Then the Spanish conquered the Incas, and the spud slipped from the hands of one imperialist to the next. The problem was, the Conquistadors and their advisers categorized this newfangled fleshy root among the New World's "deadly nightshades," evildoers that included tomatoes, eggplants, and even belladonna, a true killer. When potatoes made their way back to Spain around 1570, they were mere curiosities, ornamental garden plants, adored for the fear they inspired, like Venus's flytraps.

Spuds gained acceptance, like so much else, through a mistake. About seventy years before their arrival on the European continent, Columbus and his sailors had brought back another strange vegetable from the New World: the sweet potato, or "batata" in Caribbean dialects. (If you're lucky, you can still find batatas in your market—they ooze sugar, sticky blots of it, from punctures in their skins. Terrific roasted, they are surprisingly light and fluffy, almost dry.) The sweet potato had become something of a fad in Spain—it was too sweet to be evil, apparently, and certainly not associated with those devil-worshipping Incas.

After the spud had settled a few years in the Old World, some brave soul made the logical leap that if sweet potatoes were good, that other thing from the ground must be, too. (In case you're wondering, the mistake was thinking that sweet potatoes and potatoes were just different versions of each other. They're not. More on that later.) For no scientific reason the two foods were both named "potato," leading to endless confusion.

The spud flashed across Europe during the Enlightenment as a marvel of social engineering, a quick fix for famines, a cheap way to feed the poor. Germany was soon converted, then Poland, then Russia. In their missionary zeal, potatoes even made it all the way back across the Atlantic to North America, only to be greeted with insults. John Adams once said he'd rather suffer the indignity of eating potatoes than submit to the British crown. But a few years later, Thomas Jefferson, ever the iconoclast, daringly claimed to have eaten—and enjoyed—them.

At about the same time, Antoine-August Parmentier, a French chemist, was released from a German pokey (where he'd been held as a prisoner of war). He made his way back to Paris, singing the praises of prison food—potatoes. As a reward for his military service, he was given a coveted plot of land inside the city limits. Naturally, he planted his favorite crop—and then, to assure its lasting acceptance, hired goons to patrol the field, as if it were Fort Knox, but told them to look the other way when Parisians began pilfering it. So began the spud's rise onto the best tables.

Today, potatoes are one of the few truly global crops. China, a latecomer to the potato game, is now the world's largest producer; Saudi Arabia has a near mania for French fries; in Zimbabwe, the spud's a burgeoning industry in a nearly ruined economy. Now cultivated on every continent in places such as Mali, India, Thailand, Borneo, and Australia, the lowly potato has truly become the world's cuisine.

Sweet Potatoes: The Welcome Interlopers

The confusion between sweet potatoes and potatoes arose because of reasoning that went like this: if two things look alike, they must be the same thing. But a sweet potato (*Ipomoea batatas,* if you go in for Latin bio-speak) isn't a potato (*Solanum tuberosum*). For one thing, a sweet potato prefers warmer climes like the Caribbean islands or the American South; a potato, chilly places like the Andes, Maine, or Idaho.

We've included those welcome interlopers, sweet potatoes, in the potato category because it's just too late to extricate ourselves from mistakes made several hundred years ago. Besides, sweet potatoes are often found in the same types of dishes as potatoes: casseroles, stews, and gratins. And they get put on the same counter in the market.

But to make matters more confusing, some savvy Dixie marketers got together years ago and decided to call their sweet potatoes "yams," to distinguish them from Yankee varietals. Nothing could be more misleading. A yam is yet another food entirely: a white-fleshed, dry, sometimes almost sour, dark-skinned tuber. Chances are, you'll rarely run across a true yam, unless you're shopping in African, Filipino, or Japanese markets. In a break for clarity, we only call for sweet potatoes in this book, no yams.

Potato Types

We've used six broad categories of potatoes because we were trying to keep the recipes in focus with the way most of us find potatoes in our local markets. In other words, our categories are not as precise as they are practical. Here's our basic breakdown.

BAKING POTATOES. Don't let the name fool you. We mean those large, brown-skinned, white-fleshed, high-starch, oval potatoes that are not necessarily just for baking. There are generics now available in supermarkets—but we prefer Russets, and say so in the recipes. In the ingredient lists, some call for "baking potatoes, *such as* Russets" (meaning you're free to use whatever generic you wish, although we like the texture of Russets); others call for "baking potatoes, *preferably* Russets" (meaning "use Russets unless you simply can't find them"). There are two dishes, Gnocchi and

Noodles with Mushrooms, which simply won't work with any varietal besides Russets.

WHITE POTATOES. We mean either long thin or pudgy round white potatoes, the latter sometimes called "boiling potatoes." The key here is their skin, which is pale white or beige, somewhat translucent, not tough or earthy. (Their flesh is always white.) White potatoes range from medium-starch to slightly waxy in texture.

YELLOW-FLESHED POTATOES. These medium-starch potatoes are now common in markets across the country. Their skins may be yellow, golden, or just slightly beige, but the flesh is always yellow. The most common varietal is Yukon Gold, but there are lots of others, like the fancy French Charlotte or the increasingly popular Ozette from Washington State.

RED-SKINNED POTATOES. When we were growing up, red-skinned potatoes were lumped together as "new potatoes." They still are in some supermarkets. Not so, really. There are many varieties, from Ruby Crescent to the ubiquitous Red Bliss, probably what most of us know as the classic "new potato." Here's what they all have in common: red skins, low starch, and a waxy texture. Most often baked or roasted, they also work well in soups because their low starch allows them to soften without clouding the broth.

PURPLE POTATOES. Probably the closest thing we have to the original potato, and a bit of a rarity, purple potatoes have begun showing up across the United States, particularly in Latin American and Mexican markets, but also in gourmet stores, thanks to increased production in California. The skin is usually purple, or perhaps blue or even lavender; the flesh may or may not be so colored. These potatoes are very waxy, almost dry, with a nutty flavor. They are sometimes sold as "blue potatoes." They can stain your hands and clothes. Work with rubber gloves and an apron if you're worried about it.

SWEET POTATOES. Most of us think of these as orange-fleshed. In truth, sweet potatoes can run the gamut from white to red, from moist to dry. Varietals include Red Garnet and Jewel. So-called white-fleshed sweet potatoes are rarities, popular in some Asian dishes.

A Word About Fingerlings. These narrow, thin varietals, straight or crooked, have begun showing up in American markets, a boon to potato lovers everywhere. Their name actually has nothing to do with fingers but was originally applied in Germany because they look like small thin fish, or fingerlings. They cross most of our categories: white, yellow-fleshed, red-skinned, or purple. They often have a somewhat more "compact" or drier texture than their round counterparts; some are quite nutty in flavor.

Buying and Storing Potatoes

BUY POTATOES OF SIMILAR SIZES. They'll cook at the same rate.

BUY POTATOES WITH FIRM SKINS. If the skins are loose on the flesh or (worse yet) mushy, forget about it. The potatoes are old, they've been improperly stored, and they're not worth the hassle of peeling around the bad parts.

DON'T REFRIGERATE POTATOES. Once harvested, potatoes are fragile. The starch will break down into simple sugars if the potato is kept below 40°F. Store potatoes in a dark, cool place—but not near the onions, whose fumes can speed up the decay of potato flesh.

DON'T STORE POTATOES IN A PLASTIC BAG. You'll get a little ecosystem going in there. Potatoes need to be exposed to dry air, not each other's dank gases. Most varietals last a week at room temperature; red-skinned potatoes last longer, about two weeks with proper storage. Russets, "baking potatoes," and some whites can last up to ten months, if stored in dry, cool, dark places.

AVOID THE GAMY GREEN BITS. All potatoes, but particularly white and yellow-fleshed ones, are susceptible to green spots caused by alkaloids blooming in the flesh. These chemicals are actually toxic if eaten in large doses. Avoid the greening of your spuds by keeping them out of the light. Or do what we do—buy potatoes as you need them. You may cut out the green spots; but once they begin, they compromise the entire potato, their chemical threads extending throughout the flesh.

Tips for Working with Potatoes

THE EYES DON'T HAVE IT. Cut out any sprouts, making a small well around them.

SCRUB THE POTATOES. Ideally, your potatoes will be so fresh, they'll still have dirt clumped on the skins. Even if you don't see any, there's still a film of dust. Scrub potatoes with a vegetable scrubber or a stiff-bristled brush. But don't dig down into the potato, tearing the flesh.

IF YOU'RE WORKING AHEAD, COVER ANY PEELED OR CUT POTATOES WITH WATER IN A BOWL. Potatoes, particularly baking and white potatoes, turn brown when cut and exposed to the air. Our advice is to peel them just when you need them, as indicated in the recipe, usually while a pot of salted water is coming to a boil. But if you want to work ahead, drop the cut potatoes into a bowl of cold water. Be forewarned: This extra step will often change the texture of potatoes. Sometimes, however, peeling and putting potatoes in a bowl of cold water is a necessary step, as you'll see in some recipes. In these cases, we want to leach some of the starch out of the potatoes before adding them to the dish.

BOIL THEM WITH OR WITHOUT THE SKINS. Follow the recipe on this one. Sometimes the skin is necessary to protect the flesh, so that it's not waterlogged. At other times, the peeled flesh should be exposed to the water, so that the potatoes carry extra moisture into the dish. By the way, it's a misconception that the vitamins are located in a potato's skin—they're actually bunched together about half an inch below the surface.

STIR THE STEWS FREQUENTLY. Potatoes release their starch into hot liquids—which is why they're brilliant in soups, thickening them without any added fat. In some dishes, we even rice or grate the potatoes, a step which allows them to melt in the stew and thus thicken it considerably (see, for example, Caldo Verde). But a potato-thickened soup can scorch because of the extra starch, so give it a good stir every few minutes.

DON'T TREAT THE COOKING TIMES AS LAW. Potatoes cook at different times based on their age, size, and density. There's no way to predict exactly how a potato will cook. We advise you to test for doneness and treat the cooking times as guidelines.

"WHEN PIERCED WITH A FORK." Over and over again, this is our test for doneness. Pierced with a knife is silly—what sharp knife wouldn't pierce a potato? But fork tines are the true test to see if a spud's cooked. Don't go crazy: piercing too many times can lead to waterlogged dishes. We have three levels of cooking:

- **firm** The potatoes should be resistant and slightly underdone.
- **tender** The potatoes should be delicate but still have tooth, like al dente pasta.
- **soft** The potatoes should be quite fragile, not mushy, but certainly without tooth.

PRESS POTATOES THROUGH A RICER WHILE THEY'RE STILL WARM. If they get cold, or even cool, they'll turn gummy as the starch sets up in the flesh. It's much better to press them through the ricer just when they are cool enough to handle. Similarly, peel them while they're still warm, before the flesh has a chance to adhere to the skin again.

A CUT POTATO MAKES A GREAT TOOL TO REMOVE A BROKEN LIGHT BULB. When those jagged edges threaten your fingers, unplug the light (turn off the electricity if it's a ceiling fixture), cut a potato in half, gently push its cut side into the broken bulb, and turn. Even if there are no jagged edges left above the socket, a potato will get out that broken bulb's base.

Ingredients and Equipment

Ingredients

CHORIZO This seasoned pork sausage is popular in Mexican and Spanish cooking. Mexican chorizo, or "Mexican-style chorizo," is always fresh—it must be cooked thoroughly before use. Until recently, it was the only variety available in the United States. Thanks to relaxed import laws, Spanish chorizo is now available. We call only for Spanish chorizo. It is cured, usually smoked. Because it's already cooked, it can be ordered by mail through outlets listed in the Source Guide (page 251). If you do substitute "Mexican-style chorizo," cook it first.

CORNICHONS French for "gherkins," these tiny pickles have a strong, vinegary bite. You can use other sour pickles as a substitute, but the dish's final flavor will change dramatically. Never substitute bread-and-butter pickles for cornichons.

EMMENTHALER This Swiss cow's milk cheese is slightly sweet and quite delicate. Baked in a dish, it pairs well with Gruyère.

GRUYÈRE This medium-fat cow's milk cheese hailed originally from Switzerland; now it's produced in most Western countries. Gruyère is slightly hard and aged about ten months. It grates well and is prized for its bitter, nutty flavor. It tends to mold quickly, since it's not made with stabilizers. Buy only as much as you need.

HARICOTS VERTS In French, these are simply "green beans," but the term has come to mean tiny, thin stringbeans, darker and less fibrous than their larger American cousins. In a pinch, you can always substitute standard green beans, but cut them into two- or three-inch sections before proceeding with the recipe.

HERBS We call only for fresh in the recipes. If you're using dried, use half the amount called for. Check your dried herbs periodically. Even if stored in a cool, dark place, most are of no use after three months. After that, they take on a tea-like tang.

HORSERADISH We usually call for the bottled white root, grated then seasoned with vinegar and salt. Sometimes, we call for wasabi, a prepared Japanese horseradishlike mixture, available in most supermarkets with other Asian foods. In a few variations, we call for fresh horseradish, which can be found in gourmet markets; peel off the tough outer husk and grate the white flesh with the small holes of a box grater.

KAFFIR LIME LEAVES In Indian and Polynesian cooking, the leaves of the kaffir lime tree lend an aromatic floral/citrus taste to dishes. These leaves are not edible and should be removed before serving. Dried kaffir lime leaves are readily available in Indian markets and some gourmet stores, but their taste is somewhat muted when compared to the fresh leaves, which now show up frequently in gourmet markets. In a pinch, you can substitute half a teaspoon lime zest for one kaffir lime leaf, although the final flavors will be brighter and less delicate.

LEMONGRASS This long, dry grass is naturally spiked with citral, an oil used to make citronella candles. Buy lemongrass stalks that are still tender, not brittle; and always remove the prickly outer leaves. To release the oils, crush (but don't shatter) the stalk with a mallet or the bottom of a heavy saucepan before adding this aromatic grass to a dish. Unless sliced into paper-thin rings, lemongrass does not break down during cooking. Large sections should be removed before serving, like bay leaves.

MANGO CHUTNEY This jam-like, savory condiment is made from mangos, vinegar, herbs, and spices. The most common brand in supermarkets is Major Grey's, but it's a pale imitation of true Indian chutneys, which can range from sweet to fiery. If you can, buy mango chutney from an Indian market, or one of the outlets listed in the Source Guide (page 251).

MIRIN This cooking wine, made from glutinous rice, adds a delicate sweetness to many Japanese dishes. Available in Japanese and Asian markets, it is sometimes packaged as "Japanese cooking wine."

PARMIGIANO-REGGIANO An Italian cheese made from skimmed cow's milk, Parmigiano-Reggiano is aged in large wheels, always with its Italian name stamped on the rind. We prefer it to "Parmesan" cheese, often sold pregrated and made with oil and a host of preservatives. We suggest buying a small piece of Parmigiano-Reggiano and grating it as you need it. You can store it, tightly covered, in the refrigerator for up to two months, cutting off any mold spots that bloom in the cheese.

SAUERKRAUT We recommend buying the prepared varieties found in sealed plastic bags, usually in the butcher case or the refrigerator case of your local supermarket. These refrigerated varieties are sweeter and more tooth-some than the lip-puckering and limp canned varieties.

SEASONED RICE VINEGAR In this book, we always mean the colorless or pale yellow Japanese vinegar that flavors sushi rice. Made of rice vinegar, sugar, and salt, it's available in Asian markets as well as through outlets listed in the Source Guide (page 251). We do not call for black or red Chinese sea-soned rice vinegars, often used in sweet-and-sour dishes or as condiments, distinguished by their black, maroon, or ruby color.

SERRANO CHILE A small, thin chile that can be harvested green (in its immature stage), red, or even yellow. There is a subtle taste difference between the astringent green serranos, the more sour red ones, and the somewhat nuttier yellow ones. Use any, as your preference dictates. Always cut off the stem and discard the seeds as well as their fleshy membranes—unless you want the added heat (in which case, add the seeds and mem-branes at will to the dish). Work with rubber gloves to avoid skin irritation; if you don't, wash your hands exactingly before you touch your face or eyes. You can substitute half a fresh jalapeño, seeded, for each serrano, but the dish will have a duller, more palate-drenching heat, rather than the bright spike of serranos.

VERMOUTH This white wine has been fortified with many spices. In the old days, one of them was wormwood, or "wermut" in German—thus, "ver-mouth" in English. Vermouth comes in two varieties: dry (sold with a white label) and sweet (with a red). Don't confuse the two—use the one called for in the recipe. White wine can be substituted for dry vermouth; there is no substitute for sweet vermouth.

WAKAME This green, slightly bitter, edible seaweed is very popular in Japan. It's most often sold fresh there but rarely so here. Dried wakame is available in health food stores, Asian markets, and most gourmet supermar-kets. To rehydrate it, place it in a large bowl, cover with hot water, and let stand for ten minutes.

WHITE PEPPER Admittedly, it's a fussy ingredient, but potatoes are, by and large, white or yellow—so sometimes, for sheer aesthetics, you just don't want specks of ground black pepper in the final dish. Don't get hung up on this—if you have white peppercorns in a grinder, by all means grind away. If not, a few black specks won't destroy dinner.

Equipment

BOX GRATER This old-fashioned, nonmechanized tool can be used to grate potatoes either through its large or small holes. The latter, in fact, can be used in place of a fancier potato grater. The slicing blade, sometimes set into one side, can be used to create thin slices of potato, but it's often not sharp enough (and the whole contraption's often too flimsy) to withstand the onslaught of a one-pound spud.

COOK'S HELPER This Japanese tool slices all hard vegetables into long threads. For potatoes, it provides an easy way to make shoestring fries. Attach the potato to the shaft and crank the spud through the tiny slicing hole. You'll make endless feet of potato threads—to turn them into shoestring fries, simply cut them into manageable eight- to ten-inch strips.

FOOD PROCESSOR FITTED WITH A ONE-MILLIMETER SLICING BLADE This ultra-thin food processor blade creates papery thin potato slices, but it can also "juice" the potatoes, since the blade spins so fast. Nonetheless, it's far easier to use than a mandoline (although it involves more cleanup), and certainly easier than a knife, unless you have a sushi chef's dexterity.

MANDOLINE This French slicing tool has a razor-sharp blade set into a flat cutting surface. It's rather like a carpenter's plane, except that you run the food across the blade, not the blade across the food. A mandoline can create paper-thin slices of potatoes in no time, as well as French fries and shoestring potatoes, if it's outfitted with the appropriate blades. Admittedly, it's extremely dangerous—if you have kids, store it in a locked cabinet; and only use it with the grip designed for the food, or a special cutting glove, sold separately.

POTATO GRATER An unusual device not easily found these days, this is a long-handled tool with a fine-mesh grid over a large rectangular grating area. You run the raw potato back and forth across the mesh, thereby producing grated potatoes, perfect for latkes and the like. If you can't find a potato grater, use the small holes of a box grater.

POTATO MASHER This long-handled tool has a flat bottom, usually metal or wire, full of large holes. You plunge it repeatedly into soft, cooked potatoes to mash them. You can also use an electric mixer to mash potatoes, but here's our take: a hand-driven potato masher makes denser, thicker mashed potatoes, more like those preferred in Germany and France; an electric mixer makes lighter, airier potatoes, more in keeping with the American preference. In any event, we don't recommend a food processor for mashed potatoes.

POTATO RICER Call it a garlic press for potatoes. Cooked potatoes are put in a three- to five-inch-wide basket perforated with tiny holes; a plunger then forces the potato flesh through the holes, producing rice-like potato grains without adding air. A ricer is simply indispensable for many of these recipes; it purees potatoes without turning them soggy, airy, or mushy.

SILICON BAKING MATS These new-fangled baking sheets take the place of nonstick sprays or parchment paper. You simply line the baking sheet with a silicon mat and proceed with the recipe. Silicon baking mats do have a shelf life—they'll last only for about a thousand bakings before you need a new one.

Potato Recipes, A to Z

Here are all the recipes, A to Z (or "A to W," as the case might be):

Ajiaco

This thick stew of corn, potatoes, and chicken may well be Colombia's national dish. Traditionally, two kinds of potatoes are used: baking potatoes to thicken the stew and yellow-fleshed potatoes for texture. For lightness, we've left out the traditional cornmeal thickener. Ajiaco packs quite a punch—cut down on the Tabasco sauce if you have a more delicate palate. And make sure you have lots of corn tortillas to pass alongside.

2 pounds yellow-fleshed potatoes, preferably yellow-fleshed fingerlings, such as
   Austrian Crescents or Russian Bananas, scrubbed
1½ pounds baking potatoes, preferably Russets, scrubbed
2 tablespoons canola or other vegetable oil
1 large onion, finely chopped
One 3- to 3½-pound chicken, quartered
1 tablespoon minced fresh oregano
2 teaspoons fresh thyme
6 cups (1½ quarts) chicken stock
4 ears of corn, kernels removed and reserved, cobs cut into thirds and reserved
½ cup finely packed chopped fresh cilantro
2 teaspoons salt
1 tablespoon lime juice
1 teaspoon Tabasco sauce, or to taste
1 teaspoon freshly ground black pepper

1. Cut the yellow-fleshed potatoes into 1-inch cubes, or 1-inch rounds, if using fingerlings. Place them in a large bowl and cover with water. Peel the Russets (but leave them whole), place in a second bowl, and cover with water.

2. Heat a large pot over medium heat. Swirl in the oil, then add the onion and cook until soft, about 2 minutes, stirring frequently.

3. Add the chicken quarters and cook just until browned, about 2 minutes. Turn them with tongs and sprinkle in the oregano and thyme. Cook for

30 seconds, then pour in the stock. Bring to a boil, cover, reduce the heat to medium-low, and simmer for 5 minutes.

4. Drain the Russets and finely grate them directly into the stew, using either a potato grater or the small holes of a box grater. Stir the stew until it thickens, about a minute. Add the corncobs, cover, and reduce the heat to low. Simmer for 35 minutes, stirring often to keep the potato starch from scorching on the bottom of the pot.

5. Transfer the chicken pieces with tongs or a slotted spoon from the pot to a bowl and set aside. Remove the corncobs and discard. Drain the fingerlings and add them to the stew. Cover and simmer for 10 minutes, stirring occasionally. Add the corn kernels and simmer, uncovered, for 5 more minutes, stirring often.

6. Meanwhile, remove the chicken skin and discard; take the meat off the bones and slice into bite-sized chunks. Return the chunks to the pot, then stir in the cilantro, salt, lime juice, Tabasco sauce, and pepper. Simmer for 2 minutes, until heated through, stirring constantly. Serve immediately.

It's hard to vary such a classic dish, so here are some simple toppings for it, once it's in the serving bowls:

chopped cilantro ✦ chopped red onion ✦ corn relish ✦ diced avocados ✦ diced cucumbers ✦ diced mangos ✦ diced tomatoes ✦ grated Cheddar or Monterey Jack ✦ plain yogurt ✦ precooked cocktail shrimp ✦ purchased salsa, particularly fruit-based, like peach or blueberry ✦ sliced jalapeños ✦ sliced pickled okra ✦ sliced sweet pickles ✦ sour cream

{MAKES 4 SERVINGS} Aloo Mutar Gobi

The name for this classic Indian dish may be strictly utilitarian—*potatoes, cauliflower, and peas*—but it doesn't do it justice. It's an easy, aromatic, vegetarian supper. Usually served over rice, it can also be stuffed into pita pockets, set on top of naan (an Indian flatbread), or rolled inside flour tortillas.

1 pound white potatoes, such as Kennebecs or Irish Cobblers, scrubbed

3 tablespoons canola or other vegetable oil

2 medium onions, finely chopped

1 tablespoon minced fresh ginger

2 garlic cloves, minced

1 serrano chile, seeded and minced

1 small cauliflower head, cut into florets (about 3 cups)

2 teaspoons curry powder

½ cup fresh peas, or frozen peas, thawed

1 teaspoon salt, or to taste

1. Bring a medium pot of salted water to a boil. Meanwhile, peel the potatoes and cut them into 1-inch cubes. Add to the boiling water and cook until tender when pierced with a fork, about 9 minutes. Drain the potatoes, but reserve their cooking water.

2. Heat a large saucepan over medium heat. Swirl in the oil, then add the onions and cook just until softened, about a minute, stirring frequently. Add the ginger; continue cooking until the onions are translucent, about 2 more minutes.

3. Stir in the garlic and chile; cook for 30 seconds. Add the cauliflower florets and cook for 2 more minutes. Stir in the curry powder along with 1 cup of the reserved potato cooking water. Bring to a boil, cover, and reduce the heat to low. Cook until the cauliflower is tender, about 5 minutes.

4. Stir in the potatoes and peas. Cook for 2 more minutes, stirring frequently. If the stew is dry, add the reserved cooking liquid in ¼-cup increments until moist but still thick. Season with salt to taste and serve immediately.

Crab Aloo Mutar Gobi Stir ½ pound lump crabmeat, picked over for shells and cartilage, into the stew with the peas.

Fiery Aloo Mutar Gobi Stir ½ teaspoon ground cayenne pepper into the stew with the ginger.

Hearty Aloo Mutar Gobi Substitute beer for the potato cooking liquid.

Mushroom Aloo Mutar Gobi Stir ½ pound button mushrooms, cleaned and thinly sliced, into the stew with the cauliflower.

Shrimp Aloo Mutar Gobi Stir ½ pound cold-water or baby shrimp into the stew with the peas.

Argentinean Empanadas

{MAKES 8 LARGE EMPANADAS}

These mashed potato–crusted, deep-fried pockets were inspired by the empanadas found in Jackson Heights, a neighborhood in Queens, New York, known for its Argentinean eateries. Ours are quite large, stuffed with spicy ground sirloin and hard-cooked eggs, then fried until crisp.

For the filling (or pecadillo)

2 tablespoons olive oil

1 medium onion, finely chopped

2 celery stalks, finely chopped

2 garlic cloves, minced

1 pound ground sirloin or lean ground beef

½ cup pimiento-stuffed olives (about 12), finely chopped

¼ cup dried currants or chopped raisins

2 tablespoons tomato paste

½ teaspoon ground allspice

½ teaspoon freshly ground black pepper

1 tablespoon red wine vinegar

2 large eggs, hard-cooked and finely chopped

For the dough

4 pounds medium-sized baking potatoes, preferably Russets, scrubbed

½ cup all-purpose flour, plus extra for your hands

2 large eggs, at room temperature, lightly beaten

2 teaspoons salt

1 teaspoon freshly ground black pepper

2 quarts canola or other vegetable oil for frying

1. To make the filling, heat a large skillet or sauté pan over medium heat. Swirl in the olive oil, then add the onion and celery. Cook until soft and fragrant, about 2 minutes, stirring often. Add the garlic and cook for 30 seconds; then add the ground sirloin and cook, stirring often, just until it loses its raw, red color, about 2 minutes.

2. Stir in the chopped olives and currants. Cook for 1 minute, then mix in the tomato paste, allspice, and pepper. Continue stirring until the tomato sauce is melted and incorporated into the meat mixture. Remove the pan from the heat and stir in the vinegar. Cool for 2 minutes, then stir in the chopped hard-cooked eggs. Set aside to cool completely. (The pecadillo filling can be made in advance. When it's cool, cover it tightly and store in the refrigerator for up to two days. Allow it to come to room temperature before proceeding with the recipe.)

3. To make the dough, bring a large pot of salted water to a boil. Add the potatoes and boil until tender when pierced with a fork, about 30 minutes. Drain and cool just until you can handle them. Slip off the skins with your fingers or a paring knife. Press the potatoes through a potato ricer into a large bowl and allow them to cool for 10 minutes.

4. Stir the flour, beaten eggs, salt, and pepper into the riced potatoes with a wooden spoon, just until you have a soft, moist dough.

5. Lay a 10-inch-long sheet of plastic wrap on your work surface; place ¾ cup of the dough in the middle of it. With floured hands, pat the dough into a 6-inch circle. Scoop out ½ cup of the pecadillo filling, then pack it tightly in the palms of your hands, forming a small log. Place this log in the center of the potato-dough circle. Begin with the side of the plastic wrap that's parallel to the log's long edge; use the plastic wrap to roll the very soft potato dough over the filling. Working through the plastic wrap, seal the dough, first with your fingers, then by rolling the log along the counter or work surface. Finally, seal the ends of the empanada. Keep it sealed in the plastic wrap, set it aside, and repeat with more plastic wrap, the remaining dough, and filling, making seven more empanadas.

6. Pour the oil into a 4-quart saucepan or pot set over medium-high heat. Attach a deep-frying thermometer to the inside of the pot and heat the oil to

325°F. (Alternatively, fill an electric deep-fryer with oil according to the manufacturer's instructions; set the temperature control to 325°F.)

7. Carefully unwrap the empanadas. Lower one into the oil with a long-handled strainer or spatula; let a crust form over the roll, about 20 seconds, before removing the strainer or spatula. Repeat with a second empanada. (When you use a strainer or a spatula, the empanadas don't instantly sink to the bottom of the pot and stick. But they are heavy and can break, so be careful.) Turn the empanadas occasionally as they brown, keeping them in oil until they are crispy, about 6 minutes. You'll need to adjust the heat as you fry—raising it when they first go in the oil, lowering it if they brown too quickly. Using the strainer or a spatula, transfer them to a plate lined with paper towels to drain. Repeat with the remaining empanadas, two at a time. You may keep them warm in a 200°F oven on a large baking sheet.

For a Chinese improvisation, use 1 pound ground pork loin, rather than the beef. Omit the olives and allspice and add ½ cup chopped canned water chestnuts and ½ teaspoon five-spice powder in their places.

For an Indian improvisation, omit the olives and add ½ cup slivered almonds to the filling. Omit the allspice and add 1 teaspoon curry powder. Omit the tomato paste and add 3 tablespoons mango chutney.

For a Japanese version, omit the olives and use ½ cup chopped salted dried plums (umeboshi). Omit the allspice and add 1 teaspoon prepared wasabi to the filling. Also add 1 teaspoon mirin with the vinegar.

For a Southwestern version, omit the allspice and add 1 teaspoon ground cumin, ½ teaspoon ground cinnamon, and a seeded and minced serrano chile to the filling.

Autumn Chestnut Rice {MAKES 6 SERVINGS}

This Japanese dish traditionally celebrates the coming of *shinmai*, the season's first rice. Sweet potatoes and chestnuts meld perfectly with the delicate rice, making a warm, comforting dish that's fairly sweet—typical of Japanese home cooking, but a surprise to many Westerners. This version is not as sweet as the traditional interpretation, since it uses unsweetened chestnuts. If you prefer, use chestnuts in syrup for the more traditional taste—but drain and rinse them before adding them to the pot. Shinmai is difficult to find in the United States, so either check the Source Guide (page 251) or replicate the dish with another short-grain white rice, such as sushi rice.

6 dried shiitake mushrooms, soaked in warm water for 20 minutes
¾ pound sweet potato, preferably white-fleshed, scrubbed
One 8-ounce jar steamed chestnuts, drained, rinsed, and coarsely chopped
2 cups *shinmai* or other short-grain white rice, rinsed
2 tablespoons soy sauce
2 tablespoons mirin
1 tablespoon sesame seeds

1. Drain the mushrooms, reserving the soaking liquid and adding enough water to it to make 2½ cups of liquid. Dried shiitakes can be sandy—you may need to strain the soaking water through cheesecloth to remove all the grit. You may also need to rinse the mushrooms, prying their gills open with your fingers to release any sand. Cut the stems off the soaked shiitakes and discard; thinly slice the caps.

2. Peel the sweet potato and cut it into ½-inch dice. Place in a large saucepan or a rice cooker, along with the sliced shiitakes, their reserved soaking liquid, the chestnuts, rice, soy sauce, and mirin. If using a saucepan, stir, then bring the mixture to a boil, uncovered, over medium-high heat. Stir again, cover, and reduce the heat to low. If using a rice cooker, close and set on "cook" (or the "short-grain setting," if your model has it). Cook without peeking until the rice is tender, about 15 minutes, maybe more, depending on the day's humidity and the rice's freshness. Let stand off the heat for 10 minutes.

3. Meanwhile, toast the sesame seeds by placing them in a small skillet set over low heat. Cook for 3 minutes, stirring frequently, until golden. Stir the sesame seeds into the rice mixture, then serve immediately.

Although it's not a Japanese tradition, you can stir any of the following into the rice mixture before you cover it to cook:
1 pound clams, scrubbed (discard any that will not close before cooking or any that do not open afterward) ✦ 1 pound mussels, scrubbed and debearded (discard any that will not close before cooking or any that do not open afterward) ✦ ½ pound sea scallops, halved ✦ ½ pound asparagus, trimmed and cut into 1-inch sections ✦ ¼ pound medium shrimp, peeled, deveined, and roughly chopped ✦ one 10-ounce package frozen cut okra, thawed ✦ one 10-ounce package frozen peas, thawed

Bangers and Mash {MAKES 6 SERVINGS}

The very definition of British comfort food, bangers and mash are pub fare across the realm. The dish is simply mashed potatoes and sausage, smothered in an onion gravy. We've upped the stakes two ways: by choosing kielbasa, a smoked sausage; and by adding it directly to the mashed potatoes, so its flavors infuse the dish. If you're a traditionalist, serve the sausage on top of the mashed potatoes with the gravy alongside. In any case, have lots of beer on hand.

For the mashed potatoes
2 pounds medium white potatoes, such as Katahdins or Irish Cobblers, scrubbed
4 tablespoons (½ stick) unsalted butter, at room temperature
½ cup milk (regular, low-fat, or fat-free), or ½ cup heavy cream
¼ cup sour cream (regular, low-fat, or fat-free)
1 teaspoon salt
½ teaspoon freshly ground pepper, preferably white
¼ teaspoon grated nutmeg

For the bangers
2 pounds kielbasa, or other smoked pork sausage
1 tablespoon canola or other vegetable oil

For the onion gravy
4 tablespoons (½ stick) unsalted butter, at room temperature
3 large onions, thinly sliced
3 tablespoons all-purpose flour
2 cups dark beer such as Bass or Negro Mondelo
1 cup beef stock
¼ cup chopped fresh parsley
1 teaspoon salt, or to taste
½ teaspoon freshly ground black pepper

1. To make the mashed potatoes, bring a medium pot of salted water to a boil. Add the potatoes and cook until tender when pierced with a fork, about 20 minutes. Remove with a slotted spoon and cool just until you can handle them, reserving the cooking water. Slip off the skins with your fingers or a paring knife. Place the potatoes in a large bowl; mash them with a potato masher or an electric mixer at low speed. Continue beating or mashing as you stir in the butter, milk, sour cream, salt, pepper, and grated nutmeg. Cover loosely to keep warm and set aside.

2. To make the bangers, bring the reserved cooking water back to a boil; add the kielbasa. Cook for 10 minutes; then drain, cool slightly, and cut the sausage into ½-inch slices. Heat a large skillet over medium-high heat. Swirl in the oil, then add the sausage slices and cook until brown, about 3 minutes, turning occasionally. Either transfer the sausages to a plate lined with paper towels to drain before adding them to the mashed potatoes, or add the sausages directly to the mashed potatoes with the pan drippings. Cover loosely and set aside.

3. To make the onion gravy, melt the butter in a large skillet or sauté pan set over very low heat. Add the onions and cook, stirring frequently, until golden and sweet, about 15 minutes. Reduce the heat further if the onions start to brown.

4. Whisk in the flour and cook for a minute. Raise the heat to medium and whisk in the beer and stock, scraping up any bits on the bottom of the pan. Continue whisking until the mixture thickens, about a minute; then whisk in the parsley, salt, and pepper. To serve, pour the gravy over the mashed potato–sausage mixture.

Bangers and Sweet Mash Use sweet potatoes, rather than white.

Bangers, Mash, and Brussels Sprouts Stir 2 cups steamed Brussels sprouts, halved, into the potato mixture with the sausage.

Cheesy Bangers and Mash Stir 1 cup (about 4 ounces) shredded aged Cheddar into the potato mixture with the sausage.

Curried Bangers and Mash Omit the sour cream. Beat ¼ cup mango chutney and 2 teaspoons curry powder into the mashed potato mixture.

Wisconsin Brats and Mash Use bratwurst instead of the kielbasa. Cook the bratwurst in beer, rather than the reserved cooking water.

Barbecued Pulled Pork with Potatoes

{MAKES 8 SERVINGS}

Venerated almost as much as high school football in some parts of the South, barbecued pulled pork has roots that extend back to African cultures first transplanted to the Caribbean, then to southern plantations. This version is sweet, thick, and ever so easy, thanks to the modern convenience of a slow-cooker. The shredded potatoes melt into the sauce, making it velvety smooth.

For the sauce

1½ tablespoons canola or other vegetable oil

3 medium onions, finely chopped

8 garlic cloves, minced

2 tablespoons chili powder

1 cup ketchup

½ cup bottled chili sauce, such as Heinz

¼ cup plus 2 tablespoons cider vinegar

¼ cup packed dark brown sugar

2 tablespoons unsulphured molasses

2 tablespoons Worcestershire sauce

2 teaspoons liquid smoke

1 teaspoon freshly ground black pepper

For the stew

2 pounds baking potatoes, preferably Russets, scrubbed

One 3½- to 4-pound boneless pork shoulder

Corn tortillas, or hamburger buns and pickle relish, for garnish (optional)

1. To make the sauce, heat a large saucepan over medium heat. Swirl in the oil; then add the onions and cook, stirring often, until soft and fragrant, about 4 minutes. Stir in the garlic and chili powder and cook for 30 seconds; then stir in the ketchup, chili sauce, vinegar, brown sugar, molasses, Worcestershire sauce, liquid smoke, and pepper. Reduce the heat to medium-low and simmer for 5 minutes, stirring frequently. Remove from the heat, cover, and set aside while you prepare the potatoes and pork.

2. Peel the potatoes and shred them, using the large holes of a box grater or a food processor fitted with a shredding blade. Working in small batches, squeeze the potatoes over the sink to get rid of any excess moisture, then place them in a 4½-quart (or larger) slow-cooker.

3. Pour the prepared sauce over the potatoes and mix well with a wooden spoon. Make a shallow well in the center and place the pork shoulder in it. Cover and cook on low for 10 hours, or until the pork is tender.

4. Remove the meat from the slow-cooker and shred it, using a large meat fork, rather than a knife. If desired, skim any visible fat from the mixture in the slow-cooker; then return the shredded meat to the sauce. Stir well, then cook on low for 30 minutes. Serve immediately with corn tortillas, or on hamburger buns with sweet pickle relish.

Chinese Pulled Pork Omit the chili sauce. Add ½ cup hoisin sauce and 1 tablespoon five-spice powder with the ketchup.

Extra Spicy Pulled Pork Omit the ketchup. Increase the chili sauce to 1½ cups.

Pulled Pork and Black Beans Add one 15-ounce can black beans, drained and rinsed, to the sauce along with the meat for the final 30 minutes.

Rum Pulled Pork Add ¼ cup dark rum to the sauce along with the ketchup. Add 1 plantain, cut into 1-inch chunks, with the pork.

Szechwan Pulled Pork Reduce the ketchup to ½ cup and add ½ cup hoisin sauce to the barbecue sauce. Also add 6 to 12 Chinese dried red chiles and 1 tablespoon Szechwan peppercorns, crushed. Peel and roughly chop 2 bananas and add them to the sauce with the meat for the last 30 minutes of cooking.

Beef Stew with Duchess Potatoes

{MAKES 6 SERVINGS}

This is nothing more than a homey beef stew with a mashed potato topping. Duchess potatoes are great on their own and can also top other pot pies or casseroles. Although they are traditionally piped on, they can be spooned on with good success but far less frippery. By the way, there probably was no "duchess" who inspired these potatoes, since half a dozen have tottered out over the years to claim the prize.

For the stew

1 tablespoon unsalted butter

½ pound bacon, cut into ½-inch pieces

2 pounds beef chuck, or beef stew meat, cut into 1½-inch chunks

2 large onions, chopped

4 garlic cloves, minced

2 tablespoons all-purpose flour

2 cups beef stock

1 cup red wine

2 bay leaves

2 teaspoons fresh thyme

2 teaspoons chopped fresh rosemary

2 tablespoons red currant jelly

½ teaspoon salt, or to taste

For the Duchess potatoes

2 pounds medium baking potatoes, preferably Russets, scrubbed

¾ cup heavy cream

4 tablespoons (½ stick) unsalted butter, at room temperature

5 large egg yolks, at room temperature

½ teaspoon salt

½ teaspoon ground white pepper (optional)

1. To make the stew, position the rack in the middle of the oven and preheat the oven to 350°F.

2. Melt the butter in a large oven-safe pot or a Dutch oven set over medium-high heat. Add the bacon and fry it until it renders its fat and begins to crisp. Using a slotted spoon, transfer the bacon bits to a paper towel–lined plate, leaving the grease in the pot. Add the beef and sauté until brown, turning often, about 3 minutes.

3. Transfer the beef to a second plate, then add the onions to the pot and cook just until soft, about a minute. Add the garlic and cook for 20 seconds, then sprinkle the flour over the whole mixture. Stir well, then cook for 15 seconds.

4. Whisk in the stock and red wine in a slow, steady, thin stream. Continue whisking until the mixture thickens, about a minute, scraping up any browned bits on the bottom of the pot.

5. Return the meat, any accumulated juices, and the bacon to the pot; stir in the bay leaves, thyme, and rosemary. Cover and bake for 1 hour 30 minutes, or until the beef is tender.

6. Meanwhile, to make the Duchess potatoes, bring a large pot of salted water to a boil. Add the Russets and cook until tender when pierced with a fork, about 25 minutes. Drain and cool them just until you can handle them. Slip off the skins with your fingers or a paring knife, then press the potatoes through a potato ricer into a medium saucepan. Set the saucepan over medium heat and cook for 2 minutes, stirring constantly, to dry out the potatoes. A starchy film will begin to coat the bottom and sides of the pan.

7. Immediately take the pan off the heat. With an electric mixer at medium speed, beat in the cream and butter until smooth. Beat in the egg yolks one at a time, allowing the last yolk to be beaten in for 1 minute, then season with salt and pepper, if using. (If you're making Duchess potatoes on their own, they should now be placed in a 2-quart baking dish and baked in a 350°F oven for 30 minutes, or until set like a custard.)

8. When the beef stew is done, place the pot or Dutch oven on the top of the stove over low heat. (Keep the oven on.) Remove the bay leaves and discard them. Melt the red currant jelly into the sauce. Season with salt.

9. To finish the dish, you may keep the stew in the same pot or transfer it to a 9 × 13-inch baking dish. Spoon the Duchess potatoes around the edge of the stew, leaving a center hole to show the stew. You can also pipe the Duchess potatoes over the dish, using a pastry bag fitted with a #9 star or round tip.

10. Return the dish to the oven and bake for 40 minutes, or until the potatoes are brown and the stew is bubbling. Let stand for 5 minutes, then serve.

Beef and Mushroom Stew with Duchess Potatoes Add ½ pound cremini or button mushrooms, cleaned and sliced, with the onion.

Hearty Beef Stew with Duchess Potatoes Substitute one 12-ounce bottle dark beer for the wine.

Orange Beef Stew with Duchess Potatoes Add 2 tablespoons grated orange zest and 1 teaspoon crushed red pepper flakes with the garlic. Substitute 2 tablespoons orange marmalade for the red currant jelly.

Southwest Beef Stew with Duchess Potatoes Omit the rosemary. Add 2 tablespoons chili powder, ½ teaspoon ground coriander, and ½ teaspoon ground cinnamon with the thyme.

Blintzes {MAKES 8 BLINTZES}

Blintzes are little crepe pillows, usually filled with sweetened ricotta, farmer, or cottage cheese, then spiked with fruit or jam. But there have always been potato blintzes, too—perhaps not an everyday dish anymore, but certainly due for a comeback. They're perfect for a weekend brunch or an elegant late-night supper.

For the filling

1 pound medium baking potatoes, such as Russets, scrubbed
6 tablespoons sour cream (regular, low-fat, or fat-free)
4 tablespoons (½ stick) unsalted butter, at room temperature
1½ tablespoons sugar

For the crepes

2 large eggs, at room temperature, lightly beaten
1 cup water
½ teaspoon salt
1 cup all-purpose flour
4 tablespoons (½ stick) unsalted butter, or more, for frying
Sour cream, for garnish, if desired

1. To make the filling, bring a medium pot of salted water to a boil. Add the potatoes and cook until tender when pierced with a fork, about 25 minutes. Drain and cool until you can handle them, then slip the skins off with your fingers or a paring knife. Press the potatoes through a potato ricer into a large bowl. Stir in the sour cream, butter, and sugar with a wooden spoon until smooth. Set aside.

2. To make the crepes, whisk the eggs, water, and salt in a medium bowl until well combined. Whisk in the flour until smooth.

3. Heat an 8-inch skillet (preferably nonstick) over medium heat. Swirl in a scant ½ teaspoon butter until it's melted and the pan is coated. Pour ¼ cup of the crepe batter into the center of the pan, then swirl the pan until the batter coats its bottom. Cook for a little less than 2 minutes, or until the bottom of the crepe barely begins to brown. Turn with a spatula, then cook for 1 minute. You don't want much color on the crepe, just a brown spot here and there. Transfer the crepe to a plate. Continue to make crepes, swirling a scant ½ teaspoon of butter into the skillet each time, and stacking the crepes on the plate, or between sheets of wax paper.

4. To make the blintzes, lay a crepe on your work surface, place ⅓ cup potato filling in the middle of the crepe, and gently press with the back of a spoon to shape the filling into a flattened, ½-inch-thick cylinder, about 4 inches long and 2 inches wide. Fold the sides of the crepe nearest the ends of the cylinder onto the filling, then pull one side of the crepe up and over the cylinder. Roll the blintz into a small log, much like an egg roll. Flatten slightly with the palm of your hand and set aside. Repeat with the remaining crepes and filling.

5. Melt 1 tablespoon of the butter in a large skillet over medium-high heat. Swirl to coat the skillet, then add four blintzes. Fry until golden, about 2 minutes, then gently turn and fry the other side until golden, about 2 more minutes. Transfer these to a platter and repeat the process with the remaining blintzes. Serve immediately, garnishing with sour cream, if desired.

Add one of the following to the potato mixture filling along with the sour cream:
½ cup jam or preserves (choose any flavor you wish, but do not use jelly) ✦ ½ cup any canned pie filling ✦ ½ cup orange or lemon marmalade ✦ ⅓ cup chopped dates ✦ ⅓ cup raisins or currants ✦ ⅓ cup Nutella ✦ ¼ cup blueberries ✦ ¼ cup raspberries ✦ ¼ cup chopped toasted pecans ✦ ¼ cup toasted slivered almonds

Borscht {MAKES 6 SERVINGS}

Sure, it's beet soup. But at Ratner's, a now-defunct kosher dairy restaurant that once guarded the entrance to the Williamsburg Bridge on Delancey Street, a boiled potato always sat in the middle of each bowl. Frankly, without the potato, it wasn't borscht. It was just beet soup. As to whether to serve it hot or cold, see the Note.

6 large round white potatoes (about ½ pound each), such as Katahdins, scrubbed
1¼ pounds red beets, peeled
5 cups water
3 celery stalks, cut into thirds
4 garlic cloves
2 bay leaves
1 large onion, peeled
6 whole cloves
2 tablespoons sugar
2 tablespoons lemon juice
1½ teaspoons salt, or to taste

1. Bring a large pot of salted water to a boil over high heat. Add the potatoes and cook until tender when pierced with a fork, about 20 minutes. Gently remove the potatoes with a slotted spoon to a platter; cool just until you can handle them. Do not stack the potatoes, or the ones on the bottom will mush. Slip off the skins with your fingers or a paring knife. Set aside at room temperature or covered in the refrigerator. (The boiled potatoes can be made in advance and stored in the refrigerator for up to three days.)

2. Shred the beets, using the large holes of a box grater or a food processor fitted with the shredding blade. Place the shredded beets in a large saucepan, along with the water, celery, garlic, and bay leaves. Stud the onion with the cloves, place it in the saucepan, and bring the mixture to a boil. Reduce the heat to very low; simmer, partially covered, for 1 hour.

3. Strain the liquid from the beet mixture into a large bowl, using either a chinois, a fine-mesh strainer, or cheesecloth. Reserve the liquid, but remove and discard the studded onion, celery, garlic, and bay leaves.

4. Puree the shredded beets in a food processor fitted with the chopping blade. Place them in the large saucepan, along with the reserved beet liquid. Stir in the sugar, lemon juice, and salt, then warm the mixture over low heat, just until it's heated through and the sugar dissolves, about 4 minutes.

5. To serve, place a boiled potato in the middle of each bowl. Ladle the beet soup over and around the potato.

NOTE *The only question with borscht is cold or hot. You can place both the potatoes and the soup separately in the refrigerator until chilled. If desired, whisk 1 cup sour cream into the beet soup before serving it. Or you can serve it warm by heating the beet soup over low heat; you can make the potatoes just when you need them, or you can keep them tightly covered so they remain warm (although they will steam and turn slightly gummy), or you can reheat them in a microwave on high for 2 minutes. For fans of big contrasts, put a cold potato into the hot soup.*

Bubble and Squeak {MAKES 4 SERVINGS}

To make this classic British dish, fry everything in one skillet. It was said to have been a way to tidy up leftovers, but it's now just a good, hearty, quick meal. If you don't have leftover roast beef, have the deli counter at your supermarket slice you several thick slices. The dish's name supposedly refers to the sounds it makes as it cooks—although there are less decorous explanations, too.

1 pound medium white potatoes, such as Katahdins or Long Whites, scrubbed
½ cup beef or chicken stock
1 teaspoon salt, or to taste
½ teaspoon freshly ground black pepper
1 pound Brussels sprouts, steamed and quartered
½ pound leftover roast beef, or boiled beef, roughly chopped
2 tablespoons canola or other vegetable oil

1. Bring a large pot of salted water to a boil over high heat. Meanwhile, peel the potatoes and cut them in half. Add them to the water and boil them until tender when pierced with a fork, about 20 minutes. Drain and cool slightly, then press them through a potato ricer into a large bowl.

2. With an electric mixer at medium speed, beat the stock, salt, and pepper into the riced potatoes. Mix the sprouts and beef in with a wooden spoon, just until bound together.

3. Heat a large skillet over medium-high heat. Swirl in the oil, then spoon the potato mixture into the pan. Gently press it down with the back of a wooden spoon, letting it completely fill the pan. Do not compact the mixture all at once—rather, compact it slowly, as it fries. After about 2 minutes of frying and pressing, lower the heat to medium and continue compacting and cooking until the bottom is brown, about 5 minutes.

4. Using an offset or heat-safe rubber spatula, loosen the potato disk from the pan, shake the pan vigorously to make sure the disk is free, then slide it out onto a large plate. Turn the skillet over the disk, flip everything around, and set the potato disk back over medium heat, to brown the other side. Cook without pressing down for about 5 minutes, or until the second side is also brown. Slip the disk out of the pan, cut into wedges, and serve immediately.

You can top each slice with one of the following:
a fried egg ✦ applesauce ✦ beef gravy ✦ clotted cream ✦ drizzled balsamic vinegar ✦ drizzled malt vinegar ✦ mango chutney ✦ onion gravy (see page 30) ✦ pear slices ✦ sour cream ✦ thinly sliced cucumbers ✦ thinly sliced radishes ✦ wedges of Cheddar or Swiss

Caldo Verde {MAKES 4 SERVINGS}

This Brazilian stew of greens and sausage is made with kale—or collard greens for a homier version. The grated potatoes thicken the soup so much, you'll swear there's cream in it. It's simple fare, comforting after a long hard day. It can be stored, covered, in the refrigerator for up to three days—thin it out with extra stock when reheating.

2 tablespoons olive oil

1 large onion, finely chopped

2 garlic cloves, minced

1 bunch kale or collard greens (about ¾ pound), washed to remove any grit, stemmed, and shredded

1 small dried Spanish chorizo (about 3 ounces), halved lengthwise, then thinly sliced

1 teaspoon salt, or to taste

1 teaspoon freshly ground black pepper

6 cups (1½ quarts) chicken stock

¾ pound baking potatoes, such as Russet, scrubbed

1. Heat a medium saucepan over very low heat. Swirl in the olive oil, then add the onion and cook until golden, about 15 minutes, stirring frequently. If the onion begins to brown, lower the heat and stir more often. Stir in the garlic; cook for 30 seconds.

2. Rinse the greens one more time, then add them to the pan with the water still clinging to them, along with the chorizo, salt, and pepper. Raise the heat to medium-high and cook for 1 minute, stirring constantly. Stir in the chicken stock and bring the soup to a simmer. Cover, reduce the heat to low, and cook for 20 minutes, stirring occasionally.

3. Peel the potatoes and grate them directly into the soup, using a potato grater or the small holes of a box grater. Bring the mixture back to a boil, reduce the heat so that the soup bubbles at the slowest simmer, and cook for 10 minutes, stirring frequently to keep it from scorching. Season with more salt, if desired; and serve immediately.

Chicken Caldo Verde Substitute ½ pound boneless, skinless chicken breast meat, cut into ½-inch cubes, for the chorizo.

Crab Caldo Verde Add ½ pound lump crabmeat, picked over for shells and cartilage, with the grated potatoes.

Shrimp Caldo Verde Add ½ pound medium shrimp (about 35 per pound), peeled and deveined, with the grated potatoes.

Vegetarian Caldo Verde Omit the chorizo. Use vegetable stock instead of the chicken stock. Add 1 pound extra firm tofu, cut into ½-inch chunks, with the grated potatoes.

Ceviche {MAKES 4 SERVINGS}

A popular Latin American dish, ceviche is fish or shellfish marinated in lime juice until the citric acid "cooks" the meat, turning it firm and opaque. This version is a bit of a surprise—it includes pale, thin strips of potatoes, also marinated in the lime juice. The acid sets up the potatoes' starch, giving them a pasta-like "noodle" texture. It's quite refreshing, a simple supper for a summer night, or an easy lunch any time of year.

2 lemongrass stalks

1 cup boiling water

1 pound sea scallops, thinly sliced (see Note)

¼ cup lime juice

¼ cup seasoned rice vinegar

3 fresh serrano chiles, or 1 fresh jalapeño chile, seeded and thinly sliced

1 pound large white potatoes, such as Long Whites or Kennebecs, scrubbed

1. Trim the lemongrass of its outer layers, then bruise it with the side of a chef's knife or the bottom of a large pot, pressing it against the work surface. Cut the stalks into ½-inch pieces, then cut each piece in half lengthwise. Place in a small bowl and cover with the boiling water. Cover with plastic wrap and set aside to steep for 1 hour.

2. At the same time, place the sliced scallops in a large bowl and gently toss them with the lime juice, rice vinegar, and chiles. Cover and refrigerate for 1 hour.

3. Meanwhile, fill a large bowl with cold water. Peel the potatoes, then cut them in half lengthwise. With a vegetable peeler, thinly slice them, starting with the cut side, making long paper-thin slices and letting them fall into the water. Set aside for 10 minutes to leach their starch.

4. Bring a medium pot of salted water to a boil. Drain the potato slices and add them to the water. Cook until firm, for 2 minutes, or just until they turn translucent. Drain and rinse with cold water to stop the cooking. Be careful—the strips are very fragile. Line your work surface with paper towels, lay the potato slices on them, and gently blot dry.

5. Discard the lemongrass from the soaking water and stir this seasoned water and the potato slices into the scallop mixture. Toss well and refrigerate for 30 minutes, but no more than an hour, until well chilled. Serve immediately, using the marinade as a sauce over the scallops and potato noodles.

> NOTE *To slice a scallop into thin, round disks, you'll need a very sharp chef's knife or paring knife. Place the scallop on its side on your work surface and draw the knife across it in firm, even strokes without pressing down.*

Serve the ceviche in lettuce cups made from washed leaves of Boston lettuce, radicchio, or Belgian endive ✦ in chilled martini glasses ✦ alongside purchased seaweed salad (available in most Asian markets) ✦ garnished with halved cherry tomatoes ✦ on a bed of thinly sliced cucumbers ✦ on a bed of steamed and chilled sea beans (available in some health food stores and gourmet markets) ✦ in halved and seeded red or yellow bell peppers ✦ in halved and seeded poblano peppers ✦ with a drizzle of Easy Ponzu Sauce (page 193) over the top

Charlotte {MAKES 6 SERVINGS}

Charlottes first came into vogue in England in the late 1700s. They were inspired by Queen Charlotte, wife of George III, who is said to have asked for a dessert that rivaled French pastry but didn't require French technique. Thus, the new concoctions used buttered bread for the crust, rather than pastry dough. By the early twentieth century, chefs catering to New York's Fifth Avenue crowd began experimenting with savory charlottes. Those were the inspiration for this apple-and-mashed-potato bread-crust casserole, drizzled with ginger cream. For hot tomato chutney, see the Source Guide (page 251).

3 tablespoons unsalted butter, plus additional for the baking dish, at room temperature

1 pound yellow-fleshed potatoes, preferably Charlottes or Yukon Golds, scrubbed

1 large leek, white part only, halved, washed, and thinly sliced

1 pound Gala apples, peeled, cored, diced, and placed in acidulated water

2 tablespoons hot tomato chutney or mango chutney

1 tablespoon chopped fresh sage

1 teaspoon salt, or to taste

½ teaspoon freshly ground black pepper

12 slices firm white bread, such as Pepperidge Farm, left out overnight to dry and crusts cut off

1 cup heavy cream

6-inch piece fresh ginger, sliced into thin rounds

1. Position the rack in the center of the oven and preheat the oven to 400°F. Cut a piece of parchment paper or wax paper an inch larger in diameter than the top of a 6-cup charlotte mold or 6-cup soufflé dish. Butter the parchment on one side and set aside. Butter the mold or dish and set aside.

2. Bring a medium pot of salted water to a boil. Meanwhile, peel the potatoes and cut them into ½-inch dice. Add them to the boiling water and cook until tender when pierced with a fork, about 7 minutes. Drain and cool for 5 minutes.

3. Meanwhile, melt the 3 tablespoons butter in a large skillet or sauté pan over medium heat. Add the leek; cook until soft, stirring frequently, about 2 minutes. Drain the apples, add them to the pan, and cook until soft, about 2 more minutes. Stir in the chutney, sage, salt, and pepper. Stir with a wooden spoon until the chutney melts, then stir in the potatoes. Mix until well combined; set aside.

4. Cut 4 slices of the bread diagonally to form triangles. Round off the short side of the triangles, so that the slices look like pieces of pie out of a rounded pie plate. To create a bottom layer in the pan, fit these bread slices into the bottom of the charlotte mold or soufflé dish, their points to the center, the rounded edges to the rounded outside edge of the dish. Don't overlap the slices; rather, trim them to fit as necessary. Should you have holes or gaps, fill them with some of the bread trimmings.

5. Cut the remaining slices in half lengthwise to form rectangles. Arrange the rectangles around the sides of the mold, standing them up against the bottom layer of bread and overlapping them, like shingles, around the inside of the pan. They will most likely stick up over the top of the pan, but do not trim. Spoon the potato filling into the mold, packing it down so that there are no air pockets. Press the prepared parchment or wax paper over the top of the filling, buttered side down, so that it covers the bread slices. Bake for 35 minutes.

6. While the charlotte is baking, place the cream and ginger in a small saucepan and bring to a simmer over medium heat. Cover the pan, remove from the heat, and let the cream steep for 30 minutes. Strain out the ginger and keep the cream warm.

7. Remove the charlotte from the oven, remove the parchment round, and press the filling down with the back of a wooden spoon or a heat-safe spatula. Using a pair of scissors or a sharp knife, trim the bread that's sticking up above the filling, so that the top is now uniform around the sides. Cover once again with the parchment or wax paper round and bake for 20 more minutes.

8. Cool on a wire rack for 5 minutes. Run a sharp knife around the inside rim of the baking mold, then place a platter over it. Invert, then gently remove the mold. (You may need to tap it loose.) To serve, drizzle the ginger-infused cream over individual slices or set each into a pool of ginger cream on the plate.

California Charlotte Substitute ½ pound pears, chopped, and ½ pound pitted prunes, chopped, for the apples. Stir ½ cup chopped pecans into the potato filling.

French Charlotte Omit the sage, ginger, and chutney. Stir 2 tablespoons orange marmalade and 1 tablespoon chopped parsley into the leek mixture with the salt. Steep 2 tablespoons chopped tarragon in the cream.

Moroccan Charlotte Substitute 2 cups dried apricots, soaked 30 minutes in hot water, for the apples. Drain the apricots, chop them, then add them to the sautéing leeks. Substitute 1 tablespoon curry powder for the sage.

Sausage Charlotte Remove ½ pound sausage meat from its casings, then fry it in 1 tablespoon unsalted butter until browned. Drain any fat, blot the meat dry, then stir it into the potato mixture.

Smoked Turkey Charlotte Omit the apples and chutney. Stir 1 pound smoked turkey, cut into ½-inch cubes, and 2 teaspoons Dijon mustard into the potato mixture.

Chicken and Dumplings

{MAKES 4 SERVINGS}

Here's the best of Southern home cooking: stewed chicken topped with lighter-than-air potato dumplings. You must have a potato ricer—potatoes mashed by hand or a mixer can turn gummy when they steam as part of a dumpling mixture. You can top other stews and soups with these potato dumplings, provided they steam for 10 minutes before serving.

1 pound medium baking potatoes, preferably Russets, scrubbed

2 teaspoons salt

⅛ teaspoon grated nutmeg

2 large boneless, skinless chicken breasts (about 1 pound), halved

4 boneless, skinless chicken thighs (about 1 pound)

½ teaspoon freshly ground black pepper

2 tablespoons canola or other vegetable oil

1 large onion, chopped

2 celery stalks, thinly sliced

2 medium carrots, thinly sliced

1 garlic clove, minced

⅓ cup plus 1 tablespoon all-purpose flour

One 12-ounce bottle beer, preferably an amber lager

2 teaspoons fresh thyme

2 teaspoons minced fresh sage

2 cups chicken stock

1 bay leaf

1 tablespoon cornstarch

1. Bring a medium pot of salted water to a boil. Add the potatoes and cook until tender when pierced with a fork, about 40 minutes. Drain and cool just until you can handle them. Slip the skins off with your fingers or a paring knife, then press the potatoes through a potato ricer into a large bowl. Stir in 1 teaspoon of the salt and the nutmeg, then set aside.

2. Season the chicken breasts and thighs with the remaining 1 teaspoon salt and the pepper. Heat a large saucepan or Dutch oven over medium-high heat. Swirl in the oil, then add the chicken breasts to brown them, about a minute per side, turning them with tongs or a spatula. (If you shake the pan immediately after they've gone in, they won't stick.) Transfer the breasts to a platter and add the thighs to the pan. Brown them, about a minute per side, then transfer to the platter with the chicken breasts. Tent with foil to keep warm.

3. Add the onion, celery, and carrots to the pan. Cook until soft and fragrant, about 3 minutes, stirring constantly. Stir in the garlic and cook for 30 seconds. Sprinkle the 1 tablespoon flour over the entire mixture; cook for 15 seconds, stirring constantly.

4. Whisk in the beer, scraping up any browned bits on the bottom of the pan; continue whisking until the mixture thickens, about a minute. Stir in the thyme and sage, then the stock and bay leaf. Let the sauce come to a simmer, then add the chicken breasts and thighs along with any accumulated juices. Cover, reduce the heat to low, and cook for 15 minutes.

5. Meanwhile, gently stir the ⅓ cup flour and the cornstarch into the potatoes with a wooden spoon just until smooth. Do not beat.

6. Discard the bay leaf from the stew. Scoop up scant ¼ cups of the potato mixture and lay them on top of the stew. Do not cover the stew completely with dumplings—rather, let them sit like clouds on its surface. Cover and steam the dumplings for 10 minutes. Let stand for 5 minutes, then serve.

Chicken and Garlic Dumplings Stir 2 finely minced garlic cloves into the riced potatoes while they're still warm.

Chicken and Herbed Dumplings Omit the nutmeg and stir any of the following into the riced potatoes while they're still warm: 1 tablespoon chopped parsley, 1 tablespoon chopped rosemary, 2 teaspoons chopped oregano, 2 teaspoons minced tarragon, or 1 teaspoon minced dill.

Chicken, Greens, and Dumplings Stem and wash ½ pound Swiss chard, collard greens, or spinach; shred into 1-inch pieces, then stir into the stew before laying the potato dumplings over the top.

Easy Coq au Vin Substitute 1½ cups dry red wine for the beer. Use two spoons to form the potato mixture into quenelles (small, oval-shaped disks). Arrange them decoratively across the stew.

Sausage and Dumplings Substitute 2 pounds chicken sausage, cut into 1-inch pieces, for the breasts and thighs.

Shrimp, Chicken, and Dumplings Before laying the dumplings on top of the stew, stir in ½ pound medium shrimp (about 35 per pound), peeled and deveined.

Summery Chicken and Dumplings Substitute 1½ cups white wine or vermouth for the beer.

Turkey and Dumplings Substitute 2 pounds boneless, skinless turkey breast meat, cut into large chunks, for the chicken.

Chili Fries {MAKES 4 SERVINGS}

Look no further for the ultimate Texas comfort food: an easy, bean-free chili poured over steak fries. (As they say in Texas, "If you know beans about chili, you know chili doesn't have beans.") If you want, you can always prepare these oven-roasted fries on their own to accompany any roasted or grilled meat or fish. (If you're looking for French fries, see Fish and Chips, page 75.)

For the steak fries

2 pounds large baking potatoes, preferably 2 large Russets, scrubbed

1 teaspoon salt, or to taste

½ teaspoon freshly ground black pepper

1 teaspoon chili powder (optional)

½ teaspoon ground cinnamon (optional)

½ teaspoon ground cumin (optional)

¼ teaspoon ground cayenne pepper (optional)

3 tablespoons olive oil

For the chili

2 tablespoons canola or other vegetable oil

1 large onion, finely chopped

1 medium green bell pepper, cored, seeded, and roughly chopped

2 garlic cloves, minced

1½ pounds lean ground beef

¼ cup chili powder

1 tablespoon chopped fresh basil

½ teaspoon celery seed

½ teaspoon ground cumin

One 28-ounce can diced tomatoes, or whole tomatoes, diced, their juice reserved

2 bay leaves

1 teaspoon salt, or to taste

½ teaspoon freshly ground black pepper

1. To make the steak fries, position the rack in the lower third of the oven and preheat the oven to 450°F. Cut the potatoes into halves lengthwise, then slice each half lengthwise into four thick wedges. Place the slices in a large bowl and season with salt and pepper and any other spices, if desired. Drizzle the oil over them and toss to coat, then place in a roasting pan or on a large baking sheet, skin side down, so that they are "rocking" on their rounded sides. Roast for 30 minutes, until the skins begin to crisp. Knock them over onto a cut side with a wooden spoon or spatula; continue roasting for 15 minutes. Gently turn them with a metal spatula onto their "unbrowned" side and roast for an additional 15 minutes.

2. While the fries are roasting, make the chili. Heat a large saucepan over medium heat and swirl in the oil, then add the onion and bell pepper. Cook until soft, stirring often, about 2 minutes, Add the garlic and cook for 30 seconds; then add the ground beef and cook just until it browns, about 2 minutes, stirring constantly.

3. Add the chili powder, basil, celery seed, and cumin. Cook until fragrant, about 20 seconds, then add the tomatoes and bay leaves, stirring up any browned bits on the bottom of the pan. Bring to a boil, reduce the heat to low, and simmer, partially covered, for about an hour, stirring often. If the chili gets too thick, add water in ½-cup increments to thin it out. Discard the bay leaves and season with salt and pepper. To serve, place a quarter of the steak fries on a plate, then cover with chili.

Top with any of these:
canned tomatillo sauce ✦ chopped avocados ✦ chopped cilantro ✦ diced tomatoes ✦ minced red onion or thinly sliced red onion rings ✦ purchased salsa ✦ shredded carrots ✦ shredded Cheddar, Colby, or Monterey Jack ✦ sliced green or black olives ✦ sliced jalapeño peppers ✦ sour cream ✦ plain yogurt

Clam Bake {MAKES 4 SERVINGS}

After trying many versions of this beach favorite at home—some with messy results—we came across James Peterson's tip to use Chinese bamboo steamers for a clam bake. Use wide, 12- or even 18-inch steamers; in any case, you need deep pots exactly the diameter of the steamers you use. (Deep pots will hold enough water so that it won't evaporate in fifteen minutes.)

1 cup dried wakame, preferably wide cut (see page 13)
36 small clams, such as Littlenecks or Pismos, scrubbed
1 pound large shrimp (about 16 per pound), shells on but deveined
4 ears of corn, cut in half
1½ pounds small red-skinned potatoes, such as Red Blisses or Ruby Crescents, scrubbed and cut into 1-inch chunks
1 cup bottled cocktail sauce, for garnish
8 tablespoons (1 stick) unsalted butter, melted, for garnish

1. Rehydrate the wakame by placing it in a large bowl and covering it with hot water. Soak for 5 minutes, then drain. Divide the wakame among the bottoms of the steamers you'll be using.

2. Fill the steamers with the clams, shrimp, corn, and potatoes. (Discard any clams that do not close when tapped.) Try to arrange the things so they're only in one layer per steamer. You may need up to 8 steamers, depending on their size.

3. Bring one or more pots of salted water to a boil over high heat. Place the steamers on top, stacking them as necessary. Cover and steam for 15 minutes, or until the potatoes are tender when pierced with a fork and the clams open (discard any clams that don't). Serve immediately in bowls, or dump everything onto a newspaper-covered table. Pass the cocktail sauce and butter alongside as dips.

Add any of the following to the steamer baskets:
baby carrots ✦ bay scallops ✦ cockles ✦ crawfish ✦ fennel, trimmed and thinly sliced ✦ kaffir lime leaves (discard before eating) ✦ mussels, scrubbed and debearded (discard any that don't open) ✦ red onion, thinly sliced ✦ sea scallops ✦ sesame seeds ✦ softshell crabs ✦ uncooked lobster tails, cut into 2-inch pieces ✦ yellow squash, thickly sliced ✦ zucchini, thickly sliced

Coconut Curry Ragoût

{MAKES 4 SERVINGS}

This curry was inspired by those from northern India—that is, it's infused with herbs, not heavily spiced. (If you prefer a spicier dish, see the tomato-based Curry, page 70, or Vindaloo, page 242.) Coconut Curry Ragoût, so named because of how thick it is, would traditionally have several spices hard to find in supermarkets, but we've limited the list to only one: kaffir lime leaves. Make sure you buy unsweetened coconut milk, not cream of coconut, which is a syrupy concoction for frozen cocktails.

Two 6-inch lemongrass stalks
2½ cups unsweetened coconut milk
4-inch piece fresh ginger, peeled and thinly sliced
1½ pounds medium white potatoes, such as Katahdins or Long Whites, scrubbed
2 tablespoons peanut or other vegetable oil
2 medium onions, finely chopped
4 medium carrots, thinly sliced
1 serrano chile, seeded and minced
4 fresh kaffir lime leaves
1 teaspoon lemon juice
½ teaspoon salt

1. Trim the lemongrass and bruise with the back of a knife or the bottom of a saucepan. Bring the coconut milk, lemongrass, and ginger to a simmer in a large pot set over medium heat. Cover, reduce the heat to low, and cook for 15 minutes. Meanwhile, peel and quarter the potatoes.

2. Discard the lemongrass and ginger, then add the potatoes to the coconut milk. Cover and simmer for 10 more minutes. Transfer the potatoes with a slotted spoon to a large bowl; set aside, reserving the coconut milk.

3. Heat a large saucepan or sauté pan over medium heat. Swirl in the oil, then add the onions and carrots. Cook just until the onions are translucent, about a minute, stirring frequently. Add the chile and kaffir lime leaves. Reduce the heat to very low and continue cooking for 7 minutes, stirring often, until the onions turn golden.

4. Add the cooked potatoes. Stir the mixture, carefully breaking the potatoes into large chunks, but do not mash them. Cook for 2 minutes, until heated through.

5. Add the coconut milk to the pan. Stir in the lemon juice and salt; cook for 2 minutes. Discard the kaffir lime leaves and serve.

This stew is best served with a variety of toppings, which can be added by each diner to taste. For 4 servings, these toppings might include any of the following: 1 cup chopped apples ✦ 1 cup chopped mango ✦ ½ cup chopped parsley ✦ ½ cup chopped toasted pecans ✦ 1 cup chopped tomatoes ✦ 1 cup fresh peas ✦ 1 cup sliced bananas ✦ 1 cup snow peas ✦ 1 cup yogurt ✦ ½ cup raisins or currants ✦ ½ cup slivered almonds ✦ ½ cup toasted shredded coconut

Cod Cakes {MAKES 18 CAKES}

If you know anything about cod cakes, you're probably already asking yourself, "Fresh cod in cod cakes?" True, salt cod is more typical for these fried delights, but you can see them made with fresh cod in towns along the southern coast of Spain. Fresh cod gives the cakes a brighter taste—and frankly is far easier to find here. Panko are Japanese bread crumbs. They are coarser than Italian, British, or American varieties, so they fry up crisper. You can find them in Asian markets as well as gourmet grocery stores. In a pinch, substitute plain dried bread crumbs.

¾ pound cod fillet, cut into 2 or 3 large pieces
1½ pounds baking potatoes, such as Russets, scrubbed
1 small onion, thinly sliced
1 celery stalk, sliced
1 large egg, at room temperature, lightly beaten
1½ teaspoons salt, or to taste
½ teaspoon freshly ground black pepper
2 to 3 cups panko, or plain dried bread crumbs
About 8 cups canola or other vegetable oil, for frying

1. Bring a medium pot of salted water to a boil over high heat. Add the cod fillets and poach just until they begin to flake, about 3 minutes. Carefully transfer them with a slotted spoon to a plate and set aside. (Keep the water boiling.)

2. Peel the potatoes and cut them into 2-inch cubes. Add them, along with the onion and celery, to the pot. Cook until the potatoes are tender when pierced with a fork, about 15 minutes. Drain the vegetables, then place them in a large bowl and mash together, using either a potato masher or two forks. Let cool for 10 minutes.

3. Flake the cod into the potato mixture; add the beaten egg, salt, and pepper. Stir gently, just until combined, not until smooth.

4. Spread the panko on a large plate. Dust your hands with flour and scoop out a scant ⅓ cup of the potato mixture. Form it into a 3- to 4-inch-diameter patty in your palms, then lay it in the bread crumbs. Coat it on all sides, even rolling the edges through the crumbs. You may need to press gently to get the crumbs to adhere. Set the cake aside and repeat until all the potato mixture has been formed into cakes and coated with crumbs.

5. Pour the oil into a large skillet or a high-sided sauté pan at least 4 inches deep and 10 inches in diameter; the oil should be at least 1½ inches deep but reach no more than halfway up the sides of the pan. Attach a deep-frying thermometer to the inside of the pan, then heat the oil over medium-high heat to 350°F. Alternatively, fill an electric deep-fryer with oil according to the manufacturer's instructions; set the temperature control to 350°F.

6. Gently slide two or three cod cakes into the pan. Don't crowd them—too many and the oil won't maintain its heat or it may overflow. Fry the cakes for 2 minutes, or until golden; turn with a spatula and fry for an additional 2 minutes, or until golden. If using an electric deep-fryer, fry the cakes in the oil for about 3 minutes, or until golden, turning once. Transfer the cakes with a slotted spoon from the oil to a plate lined with paper towels; repeat with the remaining cakes. Season with salt, if desired. Serve immediately.

Stir any one of the following into the potato mixture to flavor the cakes:
1 tablespoon chopped fresh rosemary ✦ 1 tablespoon dark honey ✦ 1 tablespoon Dijon mustard ✦ 1 tablespoon fresh thyme ✦ 1 tablespoon chopped fresh tarragon ✦ 2 teaspoons ground cumin ✦ 1½ teaspoons ground ginger ✦ 6 or more dashes Tabasco sauce, to taste

Serve them with any number of accompaniments, including
bottled chili sauce ✦ Easy Ponzu Sauce (page 193) ✦ horseradish mayonnaise ✦ lemon wedges ✦ mango chutney ✦ pickle relish ✦ purchased Russian dressing ✦ purchased Thousand Island dressing ✦ Seasoned Soy Sauce (page 194) ✦ Simple Tartar Sauce (page 77) ✦ Spiced Ketchup (page 77)

Coffee Cake {MAKES 12 SERVINGS}

This cinnamon-and-sugar-laced coffee cake made with potato dough is dense and chewy but surprisingly light. If you store your flour in the refrigerator, make sure you let it come completely to room temperature before making this recipe.

For the dough

1/2 pound baking potatoes, such as Russets, scrubbed

One 1/4-ounce package active dry yeast

1/4 cup granulated sugar

3 1/2 to 4 cups all-purpose flour

2 large eggs, at room temperature, lightly beaten

6 tablespoons (3/4 stick) unsalted butter, melted and cooled

1/2 teaspoon salt

Nonstick spray for greasing the bowl

Silicon baking mat or parchment paper for the baking sheet

For the filling

1 cup chopped pecans

1 cup chopped golden raisins

1/2 cup packed light brown sugar

1 1/2 teaspoons ground cinnamon

6 tablespoons (3/4 stick) unsalted butter, melted and cooled

For the topping

1 large egg, at room temperature

2 tablespoons water

1 tablespoon granulated sugar

1. Bring a medium pot of salted water to a boil over high heat. Meanwhile, peel the potatoes and cut them into 1-inch pieces. Boil them until soft when pierced with a fork, about 12 minutes. Reserve 1/2 cup of the potato cooking water in a small bowl. Drain the potatoes and cool for 5 minutes. Press them through a potato ricer into a large bowl. Set aside to cool for at least 10 minutes.

2. Allow the reserved potato water to cool to between 115°F and 105°F. Sprinkle the yeast into it, stir to dissolve, then proof for 10 minutes, or until the yeast is bubbly.

3. Stir the granulated sugar and 1 cup of the flour into the riced potatoes, then add the proofed yeast and its potato water. Stir just until combined, cover the bowl with plastic wrap, and set aside in a warm, dry place to double in bulk, about 30 minutes.

4. Stir down the sponge mixture with a wooden spoon, then stir in 2½ cups flour, the eggs, butter, and salt. Turn the dough out onto a lightly floured work surface and knead by pressing into it with the heel of one hand while pulling it with the other. Knead for 8 minutes, or until the dough becomes smooth and elastic. You may need to add more flour, but be sparing and add just enough to keep the dough from sticking. Form the dough into a ball. (Alternatively, you can knead the dough in a stand mixer fitted with a dough hook. Place the dough in the bowl, then knead at medium speed for 5 minutes.)

5. Spray a large clean bowl with nonstick spray, place the kneaded dough in the bowl, and flip it over to coat it with the spray. Cover the bowl with plastic wrap and set aside in a warm, dry place to double in bulk, about an hour.

6. Meanwhile, make the filling. Toast the pecans in a medium skillet set over low heat. Toss and stir for 4 minutes, until fragrant. Place them in a medium bowl and mix in the raisins, brown sugar, and cinnamon with a wooden spoon. Stir in the melted butter until the mixture is moist and dense; set aside. Line a large baking sheet with a silicon baking mat or parchment paper.

7. When the dough has doubled in bulk, punch it down by gently pushing your fist into its center. Turn it out onto a lightly floured work surface and roll it out to a 12 × 20-inch rectangle. Spread the pecan filling evenly over the dough, leaving a ½-inch border along the long sides. Beginning with one of the long sides, tightly roll the dough into a tube, then bend the tube until its ends meet to create a ring. Place the ring on the prepared baking sheet, seam side down. Cover loosely with a clean kitchen towel and set in a warm, dry place to double in bulk, about an hour.

8. Meanwhile, position the rack in the center of the oven and preheat the oven to 350°F. For the topping make a wash by lightly whisking the egg and water in a small bowl.

9. After the ring has doubled in bulk, brush the egg wash over its top, then sprinkle the ring with the sugar. With a sharp knife, make six evenly spaced, diagonal slashes across the top of the ring.

10. Bake for 40 minutes, or until golden. The cinnamon filling may bubble out of the slashes on the top. Cool on a wire rack for 10 minutes, then serve; or cool completely and wrap in wax paper to store at room temperature for up to two days. The ring may also be frozen, sealed tightly in plastic wrap, for up to four months.

Apricot Potato Coffee Cake Substitute 1 cup chopped dried apricots for the raisins. Substitute 1 cup pistachios for the pecans.

Cherry Potato Coffee Cake Substitute 1 cup dried cherries for the raisins. Substitute 1 cup sliced almonds for the pecans.

Chocolate Potato Coffee Cake Substitute 1 cup semisweet chocolate chips for the raisins in the filling.

Cranberry Potato Coffee Cake Substitute 1 cup dried cranberries for the raisins. Add 1 teaspoon ground ginger to the pecan filling.

Prune-Armagnac Potato Coffee Cake Omit the raisins. Soak 1 cup chopped pitted prunes in 2 tablespoons Armagnac for at least 4 hours or overnight.

Drain, reserving the prunes and Armagnac separately. Add the Armagnac along with the other ingredients to the dough after it has risen the first time. Add the chopped prunes to the filling in place of the raisins.

Rum-Raisin Potato Coffee Cake Soak the raisins in 2 tablespoons spiced rum for at least 4 hours or overnight. Drain, reserving the raisins and rum separately. Add the rum along with the other ingredients to the dough after it has risen the first time. Add the raisins to the filling as indicated in the recipe.

Corned Beef and Cabbage

{MAKES 4 SERVINGS}

You don't have to wait until Saint Patrick's Day to find yourself savoring this Irish classic, thanks to packaged corned beef briskets now available in supermarkets. Store-brought potato rolls would be a welcome addition.

7 medium carrots, cut into 3-inch chunks
One 4-pound corned beef brisket
4 celery stalks, cut into thirds
2 large onions, sliced
6 whole cloves
6 allspice berries
2 bay leaves
2 tablespoons bottled horseradish
1 large cabbage (about 2 pounds), cored and cut into eighths
2 pounds small red-skinned potatoes, such as Huckleberries or Red Blisses, scrubbed

1. Place the carrots in the bottom of a Dutch oven. Drain the marinade and rinse the meat, preserving the marinade. Place the meat on top of the carrots.

2. Strain the marinade, using a fine-mesh sieve, a colander lined with cheesecloth, or a chinois; pour the strained liquid into the pot. Place the celery, onions, cloves, allspice berries, and bay leaves around the meat. Dot horseradish on everything. Bring the mixture to a boil over medium-high heat, cover, and reduce the heat to low. Simmer for 3 hours, or until the meat is tender.

3. Gently remove the meat from the pot and set aside. Strain the cooking liquid into a medium bowl by pouring it and all the ingredients into a fine-mesh strainer, a colander lined with cheesecloth, or a chinois. Gently press against the vegetables with the back of a wooden spoon, just to release some of their juices. Don't squeeze or the sauce will cloud. Discard the cooked vegetables and spices.

4. Return the strained liquid to the Dutch oven. Add the cabbage and potatoes. Bring the mixture back to a boil over medium-high heat. Cover, then reduce the heat to low. Cook until the potatoes are tender when pierced with a fork, about 18 minutes.

5. Meanwhile, slice the brisket against the grain into $\frac{1}{2}$-inch slices. Once the potatoes are tender, return the slices to the Dutch oven, then cover and heat through, about 5 minutes over low heat. Serve in deep bowls, ladling the broth around the meat, cabbage, and potatoes.

Reduce the potatoes to 1 pound and add any of the following with the remaining potatoes and cabbage:
1 pound parsnips, peeled and cut into $\frac{1}{2}$-inch-thick rings ✦ 1 pound rutabaga, peeled and cut into 1-inch chunks ✦ 1 pound Swiss chard, washed, stemmed, and torn into 2-inch pieces ✦ 1 pound turnips, peeled and cut into 1-inch chunks ✦ 1 pound yellow beets, peeled and cut into $\frac{1}{2}$-inch pieces

Curried Mushroom Soup

{MAKES 6 SERVINGS}

Roasted sweet potatoes are perfect for this simple mushroom soup—partly because they thicken it without any added cream, but mostly because their sweetness complements the aromatic, mild curry. If you make this soup a day ahead, you'll need to thin it out with additional stock before reheating it. Mushroom stock is available in most gourmet markets.

2 pounds sweet potatoes, such as Jewels or Red Garnets, scrubbed
3 tablespoons unsalted butter
1 large onion, chopped
2 garlic cloves, minced
1 pound cremini or button mushrooms, cleaned and thinly sliced
1 teaspoon ground ginger
¾ teaspoon ground cumin
¾ teaspoon ground coriander
¾ teaspoon ground cinnamon
½ teaspoon dry mustard
¼ cup dry vermouth or white wine
1½ teaspoons salt, or to taste
1 teaspoon freshly ground black pepper
6 cups (1½ quarts) mushroom, vegetable, or chicken stock

1. Position the rack in the center of the oven and preheat the oven to 400°F. Place the sweet potatoes on a baking sheet and roast until soft, about an hour. Set aside to cool.

2. Meanwhile, heat a large saucepan over medium heat. Melt the butter, then add the onion. Cook until fragrant, about 3 minutes, stirring frequently. Add the garlic and cook for 30 seconds. Add the mushrooms and cook until they release their liquid, stirring frequently. Continue cooking until the pan is almost dry, about 5 minutes, stirring once or twice.

3. Stir in the ginger, cumin, coriander, cinnamon, and dry mustard with a wooden spoon; cook for 30 seconds, stirring constantly. Add the vermouth, salt, and pepper, stirring up any browned bits on the bottom of the pan. Add the stock and bring to a simmer. Cover, reduce the heat to low, and cook for 5 minutes.

4. Meanwhile, peel the sweet potatoes and place them in a medium bowl. Mash them with a potato masher or the back of a wooden spoon until smooth.

5. After the soup has simmered for 5 minutes, add the mashed sweet potatoes and stir with a wooden spoon until they melt into the soup, about 2 minutes. Cover and continue simmering for 15 minutes, stirring occasionally. Season with more salt, if desired, then serve immediately.

Curried Mushroom Noodle Soup Increase the stock to 8 cups. Stir in ½ pound dried pasta, such as bowties or penne, cooked according to package instructions, into the soup with the sweet potatoes.

Curried Wild Mushroom Soup Substitute 1 pound black trumpet, hedgehog, lobster, portobello, or hen of the woods mushrooms, or any combination, cleaned and sliced, for the cremini or button mushrooms.

Hot and Sour Curried Mushroom Soup Omit the vermouth. Add ¼ cup cider vinegar instead. Stir ½ pound extra firm tofu, cut into ½-inch cubes, into the soup with the mashed sweet potatoes.

Japanese Curried Mushroom Soup Use 1 pound shiitake mushrooms, stemmed, cleaned, and sliced, instead of the button mushrooms. Omit the cumin and increase the ginger to 2 teaspoons. Omit the vermouth and use sake instead.

Sweet and Spicy Curried Mushroom Soup Add 2 tablespoons honey with the vermouth.

Curry {MAKES 4 SERVINGS}

This curry is quite fiery—typical of those found in southern India. It's tomato-based, so it's bright and summery, despite its heat. Rather than using store-bought curry powder, a tasteless extraction cut with too much turmeric, this recipe builds a traditional spice mélange in the dish. Curry powder, after all, is just a blend of dried spices—some blends are closely guarded secrets; others idiosyncratic to particular markets or religious compounds. In this case, adjust the cayenne to your taste.

3 tablespoons canola or other vegetable oil

2 medium onions, finely chopped

2 garlic cloves, minced

1 teaspoon ground coriander

1 teaspoon ground cumin

1 teaspoon ground ginger

1 teaspoon salt, or to taste

¾ teaspoon ground cinnamon

½ teaspoon dry mustard

¼ teaspoon ground cayenne pepper, or to taste

One 28-ounce can diced tomatoes, or whole tomatoes, diced, their juice reserved

1½ pounds yellow-fleshed potatoes, preferably fingerlings like Peanuts, Rattes, or Russian Bananas, scrubbed

One 15½-ounce can chickpeas, drained and rinsed

1 teaspoon lemon juice

1. Heat a large saucepan over medium heat. Swirl in the oil, then add the onions and cook until soft and fragrant, about 3 minutes, stirring frequently. Add the garlic and cook for 30 seconds. Add the coriander, cumin, ginger, salt, cinnamon, dry mustard, and cayenne; cook just until fragrant, about 20 seconds, stirring constantly. Be careful—the volatilized cayenne oils can burn your eyes. Pour in the tomatoes and their juice. Reduce the heat to low, cover, and simmer for 5 minutes.

2. Meanwhile, cut the potatoes into ½-inch-thick disks, if using fingerlings, or ½-inch cubes; add these and the drained chickpeas to the stew. Cover and simmer until the potatoes are tender when pierced with a fork, about 7 minutes. Stir in the lemon juice. If the stew is too wet, simmer, uncovered, for an additional 5 minutes. Season with more salt, if desired. Serve immediately.

Gingery Potato Curry Stir 1 tablespoon chopped crystallized ginger into the stew with the other spices.

Moroccan Potato Curry Stir 2 tablespoons tahini (a sesame paste available in Indian or gourmet markets) into the stew with the lemon juice; increase the lemon juice to 1 tablespoon.

Potato Curry Primavera Reduce the potatoes to 1 pound. Stir 1 cup broccoli florets into the stew with the chickpeas. Stir 1 cup snow peas into the stew with the lemon juice. Heat through. Stir in ½ cup grated Parmigiano-Reggiano just before serving.

Potato Curry with Peas Stir 1 cup fresh peas, or frozen and thawed, into the stew with the lemon juice. Heat through.

Enchiladas {MAKES 6 SERVINGS}

Potato enchiladas? Why not? Starchy purple potatoes, almost nutty in taste, blend perfectly with melted cheese and aromatic spices. Buy New Mexican red chiles at Latin American markets or gourmet grocery stores. If you want an easier dish, use commercial enchilada sauce—you'll need a little more than 5 cups, or about two 15-ounce cans.

For the sauce

2 tablespoons canola or other vegetable oil

1 large onion, chopped

4 garlic cloves, minced

1 quart (4 cups) chicken stock

12 dried New Mexican red chiles, stemmed, torn in half, and seeded

1 teaspoon salt, or to taste

For the enchiladas

2 pounds purple potatoes, such as All Blues or Purple Peruvians, scrubbed

2 tablespoons canola or other vegetable oil

1 large onion, chopped

2 garlic cloves, minced

2 teaspoons fresh thyme

2 teaspoons minced fresh oregano

½ teaspoon salt

8 large flour tortillas, 8 to 10 inches in diameter

4 cups shredded Monterey Jack (about 1 pound)

Nonstick spray for the baking dish

1. To make the sauce, heat a medium saucepan over medium heat. Swirl in the oil, then add the onion and cook until soft and fragrant, about 2 minutes, stirring often. Add the garlic and cook for 30 seconds. Pour in the chicken stock, then bring the mixture to a simmer. Stir in the chiles, cover, and reduce the heat to low. Simmer until the chiles are very soft, about 20 minutes. Season with salt. Transfer the mixture to a blender or a food processor fitted with the chopping blade; you may need to work in batches. Puree until smooth, scraping down the insides of the container as necessary. Pour the pureed sauce into a large bowl and set aside while you make the enchiladas.

2. Bring a medium pot of salted water to a boil. Meanwhile, peel the potatoes and cut them into ½-inch dice. Add to the boiling water and cook until firm when pierced with a fork, about 5 minutes. Drain and cool for 5 minutes.

3. Heat a large skillet or sauté pan over medium-high heat. Swirl in the oil, then add the onion. Cook until soft and fragrant, about 2 minutes, stirring frequently. Add the garlic, thyme, oregano, and salt; cook for 30 seconds. Add the cooked potatoes; sauté for 2 minutes, stirring constantly. Set aside to cool for 5 minutes before proceeding.

4. Position the rack in the center of the oven and preheat the oven to 350°F. Spray a 9 × 13-inch baking dish with nonstick spray.

5. Lay a tortilla on your work surface. Spoon a scant ¾ cup of the potato mixture down the tortilla's center axis, then top with ¼ cup cheese. Roll the tortilla up and place it, seam side down, in the prepared baking dish. Repeat with the remaining tortillas, filling, and cheese.

6. Pour the chile sauce evenly over the enchiladas in the dish, then bake for 25 minutes, or until the sauce is thick and bubbling. Let the dish cool on a wire rack for 5 minutes, then serve.

Blue Cheese Potato Enchiladas Reduce the cheese to 3 cups. Divide 1 cup crumbled blue cheese (about 4 ounces) among the enchiladas before you roll them up.

Potato and Chicken Enchiladas Reduce the potatoes to 1 pound. Add 2 cups chopped, cooked chicken to the potato mixture.

Shrimp Potato Enchiladas Reduce the potatoes to 1 pound. Add 1 pound medium shrimp, peeled, deveined, and chopped, to the potato mixture. Shrimp will thoroughly cook in 25 minutes.

Sweet Potato Enchiladas Reduce the purple potatoes to 1 pound. Boil 1 pound sweet potatoes, peeled and cut into 1-inch cubes, with the purple potatoes.

Fish and Chips

What could be better than crunchy fish sticks and fries? If you fry the potatoes in peanut oil, they'll taste nuttier; if you use canola oil, more traditional. In any case, the real secret to crunchy French fries is this double-frying method: first at a low temperature, then at a high heat. Whenever you're in the mood, you can make these chips (or fries) on their own, a great side to burgers, hot dogs, or brats.

For the chips (or French fries)

3 pounds baking potatoes, preferably Russets, scrubbed

3 quarts peanut or canola oil

For the fish

1 cup cornstarch

2 cups all-purpose flour

1 tablespoon baking powder

3 teaspoons salt, or to taste

½ teaspoon freshly ground pepper, preferably white

One 12-ounce bottle dark beer

2 pounds cod fillets, cut into 1 × 4-inch slices

Malt vinegar or ketchup as garnish (optional)

1. To make the chips, peel the potatoes, then slice them into fries, using either a food processor fitted with a French-fry slicing blade or a mandoline fitted with the French-fry blade. (Alternatively, you can slice the potatoes into fries with a sharp chef's knife: cut them into ¼-inch-thick planes lengthwise, then stack four of those on the work surface and slice them lengthwise into ¼-inch-thick matchsticks.) Repeat until all the potatoes are sliced. No matter which method you use, place the chips between paper towels to dry.

2. Pour the oil into a 5-quart pot. Clip a deep-frying thermometer to the inside of the pot and heat the oil over medium-high heat to 320°F. Alternatively, place the oil in an electric deep-fryer and set the temperature control to 320°F.

3. Fry the chips in batches, about a quarter of them at a time. If you're using a pot, adjust the heat to maintain the 320°F temperature. Fry them for 2 minutes—they'll be limp—then remove them from the oil with a long-handled strainer or a slotted spoon. Set aside to drain on a plate lined with paper towels; continue with the remaining potatoes. The chips can be made up to 4 hours in advance. Keep them on paper towels at room temperature. (If you're only making French fries, skip to step 6.)

4. To make the fish, preheat the oven to 200°F. Raise the heat of the oil to 350°F. Spread the cornstarch on a large plate.

5. Whisk the flour, baking powder, 1 teaspoon of the salt, and the pepper in a large bowl until well combined. Whisk in the beer until smooth. Dredge two or three fish strips in the cornstarch, then in the batter, allowing any excess to drain back into the bowl. Transfer the fish slices directly to the hot oil, slipping them in slowly. Fry, turning occasionally with tongs or a long-handled strainer, until they are golden and crisp, about 3 minutes. Remove them from the oil with the strainer or a slotted spoon. Set aside to drain on a second plate lined with paper towels; continue with the remaining fish slices. You may keep the drained, fried fish on a platter in the warmed oven as other slices and the fries are being prepared. Maintain the oil's 350°F temperature while the fish is frying. Sprinkle the fried fish with 1 teaspoon salt.

6. Raise the heat of the oil to 375°F. Return a quarter of the potatoes to the oil and fry them until they are crisp and brown, about 2 minutes. Remove them from the oil with a long-handled strainer or a slotted spoon. Drain on a plate lined with paper towels; sprinkle with ¼ teaspoon of the salt. Repeat with the remaining potatoes in 3 batches. Serve the fish and chips immediately, with malt vinegar or ketchup as garnish, if desired.

SAUCES

If you want to forgo the suggested malt vinegar or ketchup, try these:

Simple Tartar Sauce {MAKES ABOUT 1¼ CUPS}

In a medium bowl, whisk together 1 cup mayonnaise (regular, low-fat, or fat-free), 1 tablespoon finely chopped parsley, 1 tablespoon minced scallions, 1 tablespoon chopped dill, and 1 tablespoon minced capers.

Spiced Ketchup {MAKES ABOUT 1 CUP}

In a medium bowl, whisk together 1 cup ketchup, ½ teaspoon ground cumin, ½ teaspoon ground coriander, ¼ teaspoon ground cinnamon, ¼ teaspoon ground ginger, and ⅛ teaspoon ground cayenne pepper.

Focaccia {MAKES 6 SERVINGS}

Focaccia is a chewy, yeasty, bread-like pizza, often topped with cheese, tomatoes, olives, and herbs. In Italy, it's usually eaten as a snack in the late afternoon, in that long lag time between lunch around noon and dinner after nine. With potatoes, focaccia becomes hearty enough to be a meal in itself—although you still might want to try it in the lag between meals.

For the dough

¼ cup dry vermouth

One ¼-ounce package active dry yeast

1 teaspoon salt

¼ cup olive oil, plus additional for the bowl and baking sheet

1 cup lukewarm water

4 cups all-purpose flour, plus additional for dusting

For the topping

1 pound small red-skinned potatoes, such as Red Blisses or Desirées, scrubbed

3 tablespoons plus 1 teaspoon olive oil

2 teaspoons salt, preferably coarse-grained or kosher

1 large onion, thinly sliced

2 tablespoons chopped fresh rosemary

2 garlic cloves, slivered

½ teaspoon crushed red pepper flakes

⅓ cup grated Parmigiano-Reggiano (about 1½ ounces)

1. To make the dough, place the vermouth in a small bowl and heat it in a microwave on high for no more than 30 seconds, just until it is between 105°F and 115°F. Sprinkle the yeast over the vermouth, stir to dissolve, and proof for 5 minutes, until the yeast is bubbly.

2. Stir the yeast mixture, salt, the ¼ cup olive oil, the lukewarm water, and 1 cup of the flour together in a large bowl. Mix well with a wooden spoon, then add the remaining flour ½ cup at a time, until the mixture becomes a smooth dough. (Alternatively, you can place the yeast mixture, salt, olive oil, water, and 1 cup flour in a stand mixer fitted with the dough hook. With the mixer at low, mix in the remaining flour ½ cup at a time, until the mixture becomes a smooth dough, about 3 minutes.)

3. If working by hand, turn the dough onto a lightly floured surface and begin kneading it by pulling it with one hand while pressing the palm of your other hand into it. Continue kneading about 7 minutes, or until the dough is soft and elastic. Add flour 2 tablespoons at a time if the dough becomes sticky. But be sparing—you don't want it to be dry. (If you're using a stand mixer, turn it to medium and allow it to knead the dough for 5 minutes. If the dough sticks to the hook, add flour in ¼-cup increments at least 1 minute apart until a smooth but moist dough forms.)

4. Wash and thoroughly dry the large bowl; oil it with olive oil sprinkled on a paper towel. Place the kneaded dough in the bowl and turn once to coat it with oil. Cover loosely with a clean kitchen towel and set it in a warm, dry place to rise until doubled in bulk, about an hour.

5. While the dough is rising, make the topping. Bring a large pot of salted water to a boil. Add the potatoes and cook until tender when pierced with a fork, about 18 minutes. Drain and cool slightly, then cut the potatoes into ½-inch pieces and place them in a medium bowl. Toss them with 2 table-spoons of the olive oil and 1 teaspoon of the salt. Set aside.

6. When the dough has doubled in bulk, press it down by gently pushing your fist into its center. Oil an 11 × 17-inch baking sheet or cover it with a sil-icon baking mat. Turn the dough onto the prepared sheet and press it into a rectangle almost the size of the sheet. Dimple the top of the dough with your fingertips, then brush it with 1 tablespoon of the olive oil. Sprinkle the boiled potato chunks, sliced onion, rosemary, garlic, red pepper flakes, and the remaining 1 teaspoon of salt over the top of the focaccia. Lightly press the potatoes into the dough (but do not puncture its surface). Set it aside on its baking sheet in a warm, dry place to rise a second time, covered lightly with a clean kitchen towel, about an hour.

7. Position the rack in the center of the oven and preheat the oven to 375°F. Once the focaccia has risen a second time, sprinkle the grated cheese over the top, then bake for 30 minutes, or until golden brown. Let cool on a wire rack for 5 minutes, then serve.

Top the focaccia with any one or two of the following:
1 large tomato, thinly sliced (preferably on a mandoline) ✦ 1 small fennel bulb, trimmed and thinly sliced (preferably on a mandoline) ✦ 2 carrots, shredded ✦ 6 anchovy fillets, or more to taste ✦ 8 thin slices prosciutto (lay on top just before you add the cheese) ✦ one 15-ounce can artichoke hearts, drained, rinsed, and cut into quarters ✦ one 6½-ounce can clams, drained ✦ ½ pound medium shrimp, peeled and deveined (lay on top just before you add the cheese) ✦ 1 cup pitted black olives, oil cured, not water packed ✦ ¼ cup hot tomato chutney (see the Source Guide, page 251)

{MAKES 4 SERVINGS} Fondue

You don't need a fondue pot for fondue. Heat the cheese mixture on the stove over very low heat, bring it to the table, do your dipping, then return it to low heat when the cheese starts to set up. It's a little awkward—and it'll probably persuade you to buy a fondue pot—but it makes for a terrific party. Fondue is traditionally served with bread, dipped into the melted cheese—but we think potato chunks are even better.

2 pounds small yellow-fleshed potatoes, such as German Butterballs or Russian
    Bananas, or small red-skinned potatoes, such as Ruby Crescents or French
    Fingerlings, scrubbed
1 garlic clove, halved
1½ cups white wine, preferably Riesling or Chardonnay
1 teaspoon cornstarch
1 tablespoon kirschwasser or brandy
½ pound Emmenthaler, grated
½ pound Gruyère, grated
½ teaspoon freshly ground pepper, preferably white

1. Bring a large pot of salted water to a boil. Add the potatoes and cook just until tender when pierced with a fork, about 15 minutes. Drain and cool completely, then slice them into 1-inch cubes. Set aside at room temperature. The potatoes can be prepared up to 6 hours in advance. Let stand at room temperature, covered loosely with a clean kitchen towel, once they are cool.

2. Rub the garlic halves around the inside of the fondue pot or around the inside of a medium saucepan. Add the wine and bring it to a simmer over low heat on the stove. Whisk the cornstarch into the kirschwasser in a small bowl; set aside. (If you're using a traditional fondue pot, prepare and light the Sterno can.)

3. Add the Emmenthaler and Gruyère to the simmering wine; stir with a wooden spoon until the cheese begins to melt. When it is bubbly, stir in the cornstarch mixture and the pepper. Cook for 20 seconds, just to thicken the mixture, stirring constantly. If using a traditional fondue pot, place it over the Sterno can. If using a saucepan, bring it to the table and set it on a trivet or hot pad.

4. To serve, use long-handled fondue forks or bamboo skewers to spear pieces of potato and swirl them into the cheese mixture.

Blue Cheese Fondue Increase the wine to 2 cups and add ¼ pound blue cheese, such as Gorgonzola, to the pot with the cheeses.

Cheddar Fondue Substitute one 12-ounce bottle beer for the wine. Decrease the Gruyère to ¼ pound. Stir ½ pound Cheddar, grated, into the pot with the cheeses.

Sake Fondue Substitute 1½ cups sake for the wine. Swirl 1 tablespoon peeled and grated ginger into the pot with the cheeses.

{MAKES 6 SERVINGS} # French Potato Salad

This fingerling and chicken salad is typical fare for a light lunch in Burgundy. For an even simpler dish, purchase a roast chicken and slice the meat off the bone.

One 3- to 3½-pound chicken, quartered
1½ pounds yellow-fleshed or red-skinned fingerling potatoes, such as Russian Bananas, Ruby Crescents, French Fingerlings, or Rattes, scrubbed
½ pound haricots verts, or thin green beans
3 tablespoons Champagne or white wine vinegar
1 tablespoon Dijon mustard
3 tablespoons chopped fresh tarragon
1½ teaspoons salt, or to taste
½ teaspoon freshly ground black pepper
½ cup extra virgin olive oil

1. Bring a large pot of salted water to a boil over high heat. Add the chicken quarters. Reduce the heat to medium, cover, and cook for 20 minutes, or until the chicken is tender. Remove from the pot with two slotted spoons or a long-handled strainer. Set aside to cool, but keep the water boiling.

2. Add the potatoes to the pot and cook until tender when pierced with a fork, about 22 minutes. Remove from the water with a slotted spoon or strainer; set aside to cool slightly, but keep the water boiling.

3. Add the haricots verts to the pot; blanch for 2 minutes, then drain.

4. When the chicken is cool enough to handle, remove the skin, take the meat off the bones, and slice it into bite-sized chunks. Place in a large bowl. Slice the potatoes into 1-inch chunks; cut the beans into 1-inch strips. Add to the chicken in the bowl; gently toss to combine.

5. In a small bowl, whisk the vinegar and mustard until smooth. Whisk in the tarragon, salt, and pepper. Continue whisking while you drizzle in the olive oil in a slow, steady stream. Whisk until the oil emulsifies and the dressing turns creamy, about a minute. Pour the dressing over the chicken, potatoes, and beans. Toss to coat, taking care not to break up the potatoes. Serve immediately.

Add any one or two of the following to the salad:
2 celery stalks, chopped ✦ 2 shallots, minced ✦ 1 small red bell pepper, cored, seeded, and diced ✦ 1½ cups halved green grapes ✦ 1 cup cherry tomatoes, quartered ✦ 1 cup fresh corn kernels (about 1 large ear), or 1 cup frozen kernels, thawed ✦ 1 cup diced fresh pineapple ✦ ½ cup chopped dried apricots ✦ ½ cup chopped toasted pecans ✦ ½ cup dried cranberries ✦ ½ cup pitted black olives, roughly chopped ✦ ½ cup slivered almonds, toasted ✦ ½ cup slivered sun-dried tomatoes ✦ ½ cup toasted pine nuts

Fried Potatoes with Shrimp and Garlic

{MAKES 4 SERVINGS}

This simple sauté is based on one of the traditional tapas served in bars throughout Madrid, where it's an appetizer, served alongside a glass of sherry. It's so good, it deserves to be a main-course serving. That said, it's still best with a glass of dry sherry, or even dark beer.

1½ pounds yellow-fleshed potatoes, such as Yukon Golds, Charlottes, or
    German Butterballs; or red-skinned potatoes, such as All Reds, Red Blisses, or
    Early Ohios; or even purple potatoes, such as Purple Peruvians, scrubbed
⅓ cup olive oil
8 garlic cloves, minced
1 teaspoon crushed red pepper flakes
1 teaspoon salt, or to taste
¼ teaspoon crushed saffron
1 pound small shrimp (about 55 per pound), peeled and deveined, or 1 pound
    frozen cocktail or cold-water shrimp, thawed
2 tablespoons chopped fresh parsley

1. Bring a large pot of salted water to a boil over high heat. Add the potatoes and cook just until tender when pierced with a fork, 20 to 25 minutes, depending on their size. Drain and cool, then cut them into ½-inch cubes.

2. Heat a large skillet or sauté pan over medium heat. Swirl in the olive oil, then add the garlic, red pepper flakes, salt, and saffron. Cook for 10 seconds, then add the potatoes and toss to coat with the oil and spices. Raise the heat to medium-high and cook for 3 minutes without stirring, until the potatoes are crispy on the bottom. Toss with a wooden spoon, then cook until the potatoes are crispy all over, another 10 minutes, stirring often.

3. Add the shrimp and parsley; cook for 3 minutes, stirring constantly, until the shrimp are firm and pink. Serve immediately.

Omit the saffron and crushed red pepper flakes, and add one of the following combinations to the oil:

1 tablespoon chopped fresh rosemary and 1 teaspoon chopped fresh thyme ✦ 1 tablespoon fresh ginger, peeled and minced, and 2 teaspoons grated horseradish ✦ 1 tablespoon Szechwan peppercorns and ½ teaspoon five-spice powder ✦ 2 teaspoons fresh thyme and 1 teaspoon fresh tarragon

{MAKES 4 SERVINGS} # Frittata

Part of a frittata's appeal is that it isn't flipped, as an omelet is, so it's easier to add other ingredients. This one's stocked with potatoes—there's just enough egg to hold them together. For even more well-stocked alternatives, check out the variations.

2 pounds yellow-fleshed potatoes, preferably fingerlings, such as Russian
   Bananas or Austrian Crescents, scrubbed
¼ cup plus 2 tablespoons olive oil
2 medium onions, thinly sliced
10 large eggs, at room temperature
1 tablespoon chopped fresh rosemary
½ teaspoon salt
½ teaspoon freshly ground black pepper

1. Peel the potatoes and slice them into ½-inch-thick rounds. Place them in a large bowl, cover with water, and set aside. Position the broiling rack 5 inches from the heat and preheat the broiler.

2. Heat a 12-inch skillet (preferably nonstick) over medium-high heat. Swirl in the ¼ cup oil, then add the onions. Cook just until translucent, about a minute, stirring constantly.

3. Drain the potatoes, blot them dry with paper towels or a clean kitchen towel, and add them to the skillet. Reduce the heat to medium and cook until the potatoes are brown, about 15 minutes, stirring and tossing the pan frequently.

4. In a medium bowl, whisk the eggs, rosemary, salt, and pepper until well combined. Give the skillet one last shake to make sure nothing's stuck, add the remaining 2 tablespoons oil, then pour in the egg mixture, tilting the pan to even it out across the bottom. Reduce the heat to very low, cover, and cook until the eggs are almost set, about 7 minutes.

5. Uncover the skillet, place it on the rack under the broiler and broil until the top of the frittata is set, about a minute. Remove from the broiler and let stand for a minute, then slide the frittata onto a serving platter or cutting board. Slice into quarters and serve immediately.

Bacon and Potato Frittata Roughly chop 4 strips bacon, then add to the skillet with the potatoes, frying them crisp while the potatoes brown.

Blue Cheese Frittata Mix about 2 ounces (½ cup) crumbled blue cheese into the egg mixture. Top the frittata with ½ cup grated Parmigiano-Reggiano before broiling it. Broil 2 minutes, or until the cheese melts and browns.

Cheesy Frittata Sprinkle the top of the frittata with 1 cup shredded Cheddar, Asiago, Parmigiano-Reggiano, or Swiss before placing it under the broiler. Broil until the cheese melts and browns, about 2 minutes.

French Frittata Substitute tarragon for the rosemary. Whisk 2 tablespoons dry vermouth into the egg mixture before pouring it into the pan.

{MAKES 8 SMALL GALETTES} Galette

Galettes are small, fried potato pancakes, the perfect canvas for all sorts of toppings. Crème fraîche and sliced smoked salmon are suggested here, but lots of variations are offered below. Our galettes are made with sliced potatoes, not shredded. The presentation is nicer and the texture more interesting: the potato slices sear to a crunch but stay moist inside. (For fried shredded potatoes, see Roesti, page 181.)

1½ pounds yellow-fleshed potatoes, preferably Yukon Golds, peeled
½ cup olive oil
2 teaspoons salt, or to taste
½ cup crème fraîche or sour cream
½ pound smoked salmon, or lox, thinly sliced (about 8 slices)
2 tablespoons chopped dill

1. Slice the potatoes into paper-thin disks, using either a food processor fitted with the 1-millimeter slicing blade, the slicing blade on a box grater, or a mandoline. Do not slice the potatoes lengthwise—you want small disks.

2. Heat a large skillet (preferably nonstick) over medium-high heat. Swirl in 1 tablespoon of the olive oil, then build a galette in the pan, using 6 to 8 potato rounds and overlapping them like flower petals to form a small circle 6 to 8 inches in diameter. Fry until golden, about 3 minutes, then gently flip the galette over, using a spatula. Sprinkle ¼ teaspoon of the salt over the top, then fry until golden, about 3 more minutes. Transfer to a plate lined with paper towels and repeat with the remaining oil, potatoes, and salt. If desired, you can keep them warm on a baking sheet in a 200°F oven.

3. Top each galette with 1 tablespoon crème fraîche, then a slice of smoked salmon. Sprinkle a pinch of chopped dill over each. Serve immediately.

The list of other toppings is endless, but here are some possibilities:
barbecue sauce and sliced precooked roast beef ✦ bottled satay sauce, chopped peanuts, and thinly sliced roast beef ✦ caponata (an eggplant salad, sold jarred in most gourmet markets) ✦ Dijon mustard, chopped tomatoes, and thinly sliced red onions ✦ hoisin and radish or garlic sprouts ✦ honey mustard and precooked cocktail shrimp ✦ honey mustard and sliced precooked turkey ✦ lettuce leaves smeared with mayonnaise and topped with smoked turkey ✦ mango chutney and chicken sausage, fried and thinly sliced ✦ mushrooms sautéed in butter and curry powder ✦ pimiento slices and shaved Parmigiano-Reggiano ✦ prepared wasabi and seared tuna ✦ soft goat cheese, chopped fresh rosemary, and a drizzle of olive oil ✦ sour cream and smoked trout ✦ tapenade (an olive puree)

German Potato Salad

Chunky German potato salad is served warm, the moment the dressing is tossed with the vegetables. Bacon, rather than the more typical sausage used in Germany, is our preference because of the smokier taste with the creamy potatoes. We use so much bacon, in fact, that this salad, usually a side dish, is a meal on its own.

1¾ pounds small red-skinned potatoes, Peanuts, Rattes, or Red Blisses, scrubbed and cut into ¼-inch dice

4 large carrots, cut into ½-inch rounds

1 teaspoon canola or other vegetable oil

1 pound bacon, preferably thick cut, chopped into ½-inch pieces

2 medium red onions, thinly sliced

2 celery stalks, thinly sliced

1 cup fresh peas, or frozen peas, thawed

3 tablespoons chopped fresh parsley leaves

1 tablespoon chopped fresh dill

¼ cup cider vinegar

1½ tablespoons mustard

2 teaspoons honey

½ teaspoon salt

½ teaspoon freshly ground black pepper

1 large head romaine lettuce, cored, leaves detached, washed and dried

1 small head radicchio, cored, leaves detached, washed and dried

1 endive, cored and leaves detached

1. Bring a large pot of salted water to a boil. Add the potatoes and cook for 10 minutes. Add the carrots and cook until the potatoes are tender when pierced with a fork, about 10 additional minutes. Drain and cool for 10 minutes.

2. Meanwhile, heat a large skillet over medium-high heat. Add the oil, then fry the bacon until crisp, stirring frequently, about 4 minutes. You may need to fry the bacon in batches. Use a slotted spoon to transfer the cooked bacon to the bowl with the potatoes and carrots; leave the rendered bacon grease in the pan.

3. Reduce the heat to medium and add the onions to the bacon drippings. Cook until soft and translucent, about 3 minutes, stirring frequently. Pour the onions and any remaining bacon drippings into the bowl with the potatoes, then gently stir in the celery, peas, parsley, and dill with a wooden spoon.

4. In a small bowl, whisk the vinegar, mustard, honey, salt, and pepper until smooth; pour over the potatoes and gently toss until well combined with two serving spoons. Divide the three types of salad leaves among six plates. Spoon the potato salad on top. Serve immediately.

German Hamburger and Potato Salad Reduce the bacon to ½ pound. Fry ½ pound ground beef in the rendered bacon fat; transfer it to the bowl before adding the onion.

Shrimp and Potato Salad Sauté ½ pound shrimp, peeled and deveined, with the onion until the shrimp are pink and firm, about 3 minutes.

Spicy German Potato Salad Whisk 2 tablespoons bottled horseradish (or to taste) into the dressing.

Traditional German Potato Salad Omit the bacon. Slice 1 pound bratwurst or other coarse-grained wurst into 1-inch rounds. Fry for a minute in the oil, then add to the potato mixture. Add 1 teaspoon additional oil to the pan to cook the onion.

Gesmoorde Vis

{MAKES 4 SERVINGS}

This is an African dish of colonial origins, still popular in the former Dutch colonies. Fiery and sweet, it makes a lovely meal with hot rolls and a green salad. The only thing unusual in the dish is the salt cod. Buy it at Latin American markets and most gourmet supermarkets. You'll need to soak it for forty-eight hours before you can begin the dish. If you prefer to use fresh cod (and thus try this unusual dish with a far simpler technique), see the variations.

1 pound salt cod
1 pound small red-skinned potatoes, such as Huckleberries or Red Blisses, scrubbed
1 tablespoon unsalted butter
1 tablespoon canola or other vegetable oil
1 large onion, thinly sliced
1 pound Roma tomatoes, thickly sliced
2 garlic cloves, minced
1 fresh jalapeño pepper, stemmed, seeded, and minced
1 tablespoon packed light brown sugar
Juice of 1 lemon
2 tablespoons chopped fresh cilantro

1. Two days before making the dish, place the salt cod in a large, nonreactive bowl, such as glass or enamel. Cover with at least 2 quarts water. Twice a day, change the water in the bowl, gently pressing the cod each time against the sides of the bowl to remove the salt. Be very careful—the fish is delicate and will flake.

2. Drain the cod and place it in a large skillet or sauté pan, breaking it into two pieces if necessary. Fill the pan with enough cold water to cover the fish by 1 inch. Place the skillet over high heat and bring the water to a simmer. Reduce the heat to medium and simmer for 5 minutes. Drain the salt cod into a colander, then pull off the skin and remove the bones by picking over the meat. Continue removing the bones and pulling off the skin as you flake the fish into a medium bowl. Set aside.

3. Bring a medium pot of salted water to boil. Add the potatoes and cook until still firm when pierced with a fork, about 10 minutes. Drain, cool slightly, then cut the potatoes into quarters.

4. Melt the butter with the oil in a large skillet or sauté pan set over very low heat. Add the onion and cook until golden, about 15 minutes, stirring frequently. Do not let the onion brown—lower the heat if it begins to.

5. Raise the heat to medium, stir in the tomatoes and garlic, and cook until the tomatoes begin to break down, about 2 minutes. Stir in the pepper and brown sugar; cook for another 2 minutes, stirring constantly.

6. Add the flaked fish and the boiled potatoes. Reduce the heat and simmer, partially covered, until the stew thickens, about 15 minutes, stirring frequently. You may need to lower the heat to prevent scorching. Should the stew begin to scorch, stir in ½ cup water. Stir in the lemon juice and cilantro; serve immediately.

Fresh Cod Gesmoorde Vis Substitute 1 pound cod fillets for the salt cod. Omit the first step of the recipe. Place the fresh cod in a large skillet, cover with water, and bring to a simmer. Poach for 5 minutes, gently transfer the cod fillets to a plate, and cool slightly. Flake the fish into a medium bowl and continue with the recipe.

Garden Gesmoorde Vis Stir one 10-ounce package frozen peas, thawed; 1 cup fresh corn kernels (about 1 large ear) or 1 cup frozen kernels, thawed; and ¼ cup water into the stew during its last 5 minutes of cooking.

Peanut Gesmoorde Vis Stir ½ cup unsalted peanuts into the stew with the lemon juice.

Scallop Gesmoorde Vis Stir ½ pound sea scallops, halved, into the stew during the last 5 minutes of cooking.

Shrimp Gesmoorde Vis Stir ½ pound medium shrimp (about 35 per pound), shelled and deveined, into the stew during the last 5 minutes of cooking.

{MAKES 4 SERVINGS} # Gnocchi

Gnocchi must be made quickly. The moment the potatoes are cool enough to handle, begin making the dough; the moment you shape them, boil them. Have the water boiling before you make the little bundles and have one of the sauces listed below prepared in advance. Whew—but there's a way to stay calm: make the gnocchi in advance. Dust them with flour and freeze them in one layer in a freezer-safe bag as soon as they're shaped. When you're ready to use them, drop them frozen into boiling water and cook for one more minute. *Gnocchi must be made only with Russet potatoes.*

2 pounds Russet potatoes, scrubbed
2 large egg yolks, at room temperature
1 teaspoon salt
1 to 1½ cups all-purpose flour, plus additional for dusting

1. Position the rack in the center of the oven and preheating the oven to 400°F. Place the potatoes in the center of the rack and bake for 1 hour 15 minutes, or until soft. Transfer them to a cooling rack until they can be handled easily. Cut the potatoes in half lengthwise and gently scoop the white insides into a potato ricer. Press the flesh into a large bowl. (Alternatively, scoop the insides into a large bowl and lightly mash them with a fork, just until broken up into small bits, but not until smooth.)

2. Stir in the egg yolks and salt with a fork, just until combined. Add 1 cup of the flour and stir just until a dough begins to form. Lightly flour the work surface, dump the contents of the bowl onto it, and knead until smooth but still slightly sticky, about 4 minutes. Add additional flour as needed, in 1-tablespoon increments, to make a workable but still moist dough.

3. Pull off a section of dough about the size of a small lemon. Dust your hands with flour and begin rolling the dough between your palms to form a cylinder. Lightly flour the work surface and roll the dough against it with your palms to form a 1-inch-thick cylinder, about 10 inches long. Slice the cylinder into 1-inch segments.

4. Lightly dust a large baking sheet with flour; set aside. Bring a large pot of salted water to a boil.

5. While the water's coming to a boil, place the tines of a clean fork against the work surface, back side up. Gently roll the gnocchi pieces up the fork, barely pressing down, to give them an indented pattern that will hold the sauce; they will be slightly squished. Place the finished gnocchi on the prepared baking sheet and continue with the remaining dough.

6. Add the gnocchi to the boiling water, stir once, then cook undisturbed until they float to the surface, about 2 minutes. Drain but do not rinse. Toss with one of the sauces given below and serve.

Cilantro Pesto {MAKES 1 CUP}

1 cup packed cilantro
½ cup packed flat-leaf parsley
1 garlic clove
1 tablespoon pine nuts
⅓ cup olive oil
¼ cup freshly grated Parmigiano-Reggiano
½ teaspoon salt
¼ teaspoon freshly ground black pepper

Place the cilantro, parsley, garlic, and pine nuts in a food processor fitted with the chopping blade; pulse about 5 times, until roughly chopped. Scrape down the sides of the bowl, then add the olive oil, cheese, salt, and pepper. Process until smooth, about a minute. This pesto can be made up to 4 days in advance; store, covered, in the refrigerator and allow to come to room temperature before using.

Fresh Tomato Sauce {MAKES 2 CUPS}

2 tablespoons olive oil

1 medium onion, chopped

2 garlic cloves, minced

8 Roma tomatoes (about 1½ pounds), roughly chopped

¼ cup packed shredded fresh basil leaves

½ teaspoon sugar

½ teaspoon salt

½ teaspoon freshly ground black pepper

¼ cup freshly grated Parmigiano-Reggiano, for garnish

Heat a large skillet over medium-high heat. Swirl in the oil, then add the onion and cook until soft, about 3 minutes, stirring frequently. Add the garlic and tomatoes; cook until the tomatoes break down and the sauce thickens, about 5 minutes, stirring occasionally. Stir in the basil, sugar, salt, and pepper; cook 2 more minutes, stirring constantly. When you toss the sauce with the gnocchi, garnish with the grated Parmigiano-Reggiano, if desired. The sauce can be made in advance; store, covered, in the refrigerator for up to 3 days and reheat over medium heat before tossing with the gnocchi.

Sage Gorgonzola Sauce {MAKES ABOUT 1½ CUPS}

1 cup heavy cream

¼ cup packed minced fresh sage leaves

1 cup crumbled Gorgonzola or other blue cheese (about 4 ounces)

4 tablespoons (½ stick) unsalted butter, cut into 4 chunks

2 tablespoons grated Parmigiano-Reggiano (about ½ ounce)

¼ teaspoon salt

Bring the cream and sage to a boil in a large saucepan set over medium heat; cook without stirring until the cream is reduced by a third. Reduce the heat to low; add the Gorgonzola, butter, Parmigiano-Reggiano, and salt. Cook, stirring constantly, until the cheese melts and the mixture is smooth.

Gratin {MAKES 4 SERVINGS}

Traditionally, a potato gratin is a side dish: boiled potatoes sliced and layered in a creamy béchamel sauce, topped with cheese, and baked until bubbly. We turn it into a main dish with a layer of prosciutto between the potatoes. What's more, it makes an easy dinner or an elegant weekend lunch, alongside a green salad and a glass of wine.

2 pounds large yellow-fleshed potatoes, preferably Yellow Finns, or Yukon Golds or Ozettes, scrubbed

5 tablespoons unsalted butter, plus some for the baking dish, at room temperature

3 tablespoons all-purpose flour

3 cups milk (whole or low-fat, but not fat-free), at room temperature

1 tablespoon Dijon mustard

1 tablespoon minced fresh chives

1 tablespoon minced fresh tarragon

½ teaspoon salt

½ teaspoon freshly ground pepper, preferably white

1 large onion, thinly sliced

½ cup dry vermouth or white wine

4 ounces prosciutto, chopped

½ cup grated Parmigiano-Reggiano (about 2 ounces)

1. Bring a medium pot of salted water to a boil. Add the potatoes and cook until still firm when pierced with a fork, about 12 minutes. Drain and cool just until you can handle them; slip the skins off with your fingers or a paring knife. Slice the potatoes into ¼-inch-thick slices; set aside.

2. To make the béchamel, melt 3 tablespoons of the butter in a large skillet over medium heat. Whisk in the flour and cook for 20 seconds—do not let the flour brown. Continue whisking as you add the milk in a slow, thin, steady stream; whisk until the mixture thickens, about a minute. Take the pan off the heat and whisk in the mustard, chives, tarragon, salt, and pepper. Set aside.

3. Melt 2 tablespoons of the butter in a medium skillet set over very low heat. Add the onion and cook until sweet, about 15 minutes, stirring frequently. Reduce the heat if it begins to brown. When golden, set aside.

4. Position the rack in the center of the oven and preheat the oven to 350°F. Butter a 10-cup gratin dish or a 10-cup oval baking dish.

5. To assemble the gratin, spoon the sautéed onions into the bottom of the baking dish, spreading them out evenly across its surface. Place half the potato slices on top, overlapping them as necessary. Sprinkle with 2 tablespoons of the vermouth, then spoon half the white béchamel over the top, spreading it evenly to the edges of the dish. Lay the prosciutto evenly over the sauce, then top with the remaining potatoes, again overlapping them as necessary. Sprinkle with the remaining 6 tablespoons vermouth, then spoon on the rest of the béchamel. Top the dish with the grated Parmigiano-Reggiano.

6. Bake for 45 minutes, or until brown and bubbling. Let stand for 5 minutes, then serve.

Asparagus and Potato Gratin Trim 12 thin asparagus spears and blanch them in a skillet of boiling salted water for 1 minute. Lay them on top of the prosciutto.

Bacon and Potato Gratin Omit the prosciutto. Fry 8 slices bacon with 1 tablespoon unsalted butter until crisp in a large skillet over medium heat. Drain the bacon on paper towels, then layer it in the gratin in place of the prosciutto.

Pea-Potato Gratin Sprinkle one 10-ounce package frozen peas, thawed, on top of the prosciutto.

Spinach-Potato Gratin Squeeze any excess water from one 10-ounce package frozen spinach, thawed. Sprinkle the spinach on top of the prosciutto.

Hash {MAKES 6 SERVINGS}

Hash is comfort food through and through, hearty enough to be a main dish any time of day, rather than just a breakfast side. Have your butcher slice the Canadian bacon into ½-inch slices, far thicker than the usual packaged variety. If you can't get thick Canadian bacon, use smoked ham instead. The trick is to stir it only enough to keep the dish moist, but not so much that the potatoes mash.

¾ pound sweet potatoes, such as Red Garnets, scrubbed
¾ pound red-skinned potatoes, such as Red Blisses or All Reds,
  scrubbed
3 tablespoons unsalted butter
1 large red onion, diced
1 medium red bell pepper, stemmed, cored, and diced
2 garlic cloves, minced
¾ pound thick-cut Canadian bacon, or smoked ham, cut into ½-inch cubes
¼ cup plus 2 tablespoons chicken stock or vegetable stock
2 tablespoons canola or other vegetable oil
1 tablespoon caraway seeds
1 cup coarsely chopped spinach leaves
2 teaspoons apple cider vinegar
1 teaspoon freshly ground black pepper
½ teaspoon salt

1. Bring two medium pots of salted water to a boil over high heat. Meanwhile, peel the sweet potatoes. Cut both the red-skinned and the peeled sweet potatoes into ½-inch pieces. Cook the potatoes in separate pots, each for 7 minutes. Drain each separately; set aside.

2. In a large skillet or sauté pan, melt 2 tablespoons of the butter over medium-low heat, then add the onion and cook until soft, about 2 minutes, stirring frequently. Add the remaining 1 tablespoon butter, let melt, then add the bell pepper and garlic. Cook until soft, about 2 minutes, stirring often.

3. Raise the heat to medium and add the Canadian bacon. Cook, stirring constantly, for 1 minute. Add the ¼ cup stock, oil, caraway seeds, and both kinds of cooked potatoes. Cook until heated through and fragrant, about 7 minutes, stirring frequently but very gently.

4. Stir in the remaining 2 tablespoons stock, the spinach, vinegar, pepper, and salt. Cook until the spinach is wilted and the dish is heated through, about 2 minutes. Stir very carefully so as not to mash the potatoes. Serve immediately; or cool, cover, and refrigerate up to two days.

Herbed Hash Omit the caraway seeds. Add 2 tablespoons minced parsley, 1 tablespoon thyme, and 2 teaspoons minced rosemary with the spinach.

Juniper Hash Reduce the stock to ¼ cup. Add 1 tablespoon juniper berries, crushed, with the bell pepper. Then add 3 tablespoons gin with the spinach. Be careful that the pan doesn't flame. If it does, cover it and remove it from the heat until the flame is out.

Roasted Garlic Hash Omit the minced garlic. Instead, seal 8 unpeeled cloves in an aluminum foil packet and roast in a preheated 350°F oven for 30 minutes. When cool, squeeze the soft "meat" from the husks. Add this garlic with the spinach, breaking it up throughout the hash.

Southwestern Hash Omit the caraway seeds. Add 1 teaspoon Tabasco sauce and ½ cup salsa with the spinach. Top the dish with 1 cup shredded Monterey Jack. Cook just until the cheese melts—do not stir—and serve the hash directly from the pan.

Spicy Hash Add 1 teaspoon minced seeded jalapeño pepper and ½ teaspoon crushed red pepper flakes with the bell pepper.

Hot Cakes {MAKES TWELVE 4-INCH PANCAKES}

Tender and moist, these hot cakes (or pancakes, or flapjacks, depending on where you live) are sugar free, thanks to the sweet potatoes. They're perfect for whenever you want a special breakfast, particularly on a weekend morning. A do-ahead tip: bake the sweet potato the night before. Just be sure to have lots of pure maple syrup on hand! (That'll make up for the lack of sugar.)

¾ pound sweet potato, preferably Jersey Whites or Haymans
1 cup all-purpose flour
2 teaspoons baking powder
½ teaspoon salt
3 tablespoons unsalted butter, melted and cooled
1 large egg, at room temperature
1½ cups milk (regular, low-fat, or fat-free)
½ teaspoon vanilla

Nonstick spray for the griddle

1. Arrange the rack in the center of the oven and preheat the oven to 400°F. Place the sweet potato on a baking sheet and roast for about an hour, or until very soft. Set aside to cool.

2. Peel the potato, place it in a small bowl, and mash it with a potato masher or two forks. Set aside.

3. In a large bowl, mix together the flour, baking powder, and salt; set aside.

4. Mix the sweet potato, butter, and egg in a medium bowl with a wooden spoon. Stir in the milk and vanilla. Stir these liquid ingredients into the dry with a wooden spoon, but only until barely combined. Do not beat.

5. Spray a griddle or a large skillet with nonstick spray; heat it over medium heat. Pour the potato batter by scant ¼-cup amounts onto the griddle or into the skillet, making as many pancakes as will fit. Cook for 2 minutes, or until bubbles form across the top of the batter. Check the bottom of the pancakes to make sure they're not burning—if they are, lower the heat. Flip the pancakes with a spatula and cook for 1 more minute. Serve immediately or keep them warm on an oven-safe plate in a 200°F oven.

Stir any of the following into the batter:
½ cup banana chips ✦ ½ cup chopped dried mango ✦ ½ cup chopped dried papaya ✦ ½ cup chopped dried pineapple ✦ ½ cup chopped toasted pecans or walnuts ✦ ½ cup dried cherries, cranberries, or raisins ✦ ½ cup semisweet chocolate chips or white chocolate chips ✦ ½ cup shredded coconut ✦ ½ teaspoon ground cinnamon ✦ ½ teaspoon ground ginger ✦ ¼ teaspoon ground cloves ✦ ¼ teaspoon grated nutmeg

Irish Stew {MAKES 4 SERVINGS}

Every Irish grandmother knows a version of this lamb and potato stew. It's Emerald Isle penicillin, good for everything from heartache to more physical ailments. The only problem is that it's usually made with leftover lamb—and who has that lying around the kitchen? Our version uses lamb stew meat—but other than that, it's still a dish without a lot of fandango, in keeping with its workaday roots. If you can't find lamb stew meat, buy two pounds lamb shoulder and take the meat off the bones—or have your butcher debone it for you.

1½ pounds lamb stew meat

1 quart (4 cups) chicken stock

2 large leeks, white and pale green parts only, halved, carefully washed, and thinly sliced

2 celery stalks, thinly sliced

1 tablespoon fresh thyme

1½ pounds small white potatoes, such as Irish Cobblers or German Butterballs, scrubbed

2 large carrots, cut in half lengthwise, then into 2-inch sections

2 tablespoons chopped fresh parsley

1 teaspoon freshly ground black pepper

½ teaspoon salt, or to taste

1. Place the lamb meat in a medium saucepan, cover with cold water, and bring it to a boil. Cook for 10 minutes, skimming off the fat once or twice. Drain and rinse the meat under cold water.

2. Pour the stock into a large saucepan and bring it to a simmer over high heat. Add the leeks, celery, and thyme. Simmer for 10 minutes, then add the lamb. Reduce the heat to low and simmer, partially covered, for 25 minutes, skimming the fat as necessary.

3. Peel the potatoes and cut them in half. Add them to the pan with the carrots. Cover and continue simmering until the potatoes are soft when pierced with a fork, about 25 minutes.

4. Stir in the parsley, pepper, and salt. As you stir, the softened potatoes will break apart and thicken the broth. Simmer for 2 minutes, stirring constantly. Serve immediately.

Replace the carrots with:
2 parsnips, peeled and cut into ½-inch-thick rounds ✦ ½ pound green beans, trimmed and cut into 2-inch sections ✦ ½ pound rutabaga, peeled and cut into 1-inch cubes ✦ ½ pound turnip, peeled and cut into 1-inch cubes

Substitute one of the following for the thyme:
2 tablespoons minced fresh chervil ✦ 2 teaspoons minced fresh rosemary ✦ 2 teaspoons minced fresh sage

Japanese Mushrooms with a Sweet Potato Infusion {MAKES 4 SERVINGS}

This sophisticated dish is actually an easy meal. Its elegance lies in its presentation: fan the enoki mushrooms across one side of the bowl before you ladle in the soup. Enoki mushrooms can be found in Asian markets or gourmet markets.

2 pounds sweet potatoes, such as Red Garnets, or white-fleshed sweet potatoes, such as Haymans, scrubbed
2 celery stalks, cut into 1-inch chunks
2 shallots, thinly sliced
6 cups (1½ quarts) mushroom, vegetable, or chicken stock
1 tablespoon sesame seeds
6 ounces shiitake mushrooms, stemmed, cleaned, and caps thinly sliced
½ pound enoki mushrooms, cleaned, any remaining roots removed
Salt to taste

1. Peel the potatoes and slice them into ½-inch-thick disks. Place them in a large saucepan along with the celery and shallots. Pour in the stock, place the pan over medium-high heat, and bring the mixture to a simmer. Reduce the heat to very low and simmer at just the barest bubble, covered, for 30 minutes. Don't break up the potatoes; the broth should remain clear. Remove the pan from the heat and let it stand for 30 minutes, covered.

2. Meanwhile, toast the sesame seeds in a small skillet set over low heat until golden and fragrant, about 5 minutes, stirring frequently.

3. Strain the potato mixture through a colander lined with cheesecloth, a fine-mesh sieve, or a chinois into a medium saucepan set over medium heat. Do not press against the vegetables. Bring this strained broth to a simmer, then stir in the shiitakes. Reduce the heat and simmer, uncovered, for 10 minutes.

4. Arrange the enoki mushrooms in four bowls, then ladle the broth over them. Top each bowl with ¼ teaspoon toasted sesame seeds, season with salt, and serve immediately.

Before you ladle the broth into the bowls, divide any of the following among the bowls and arrange it as desired with the enoki mushrooms:
1 pound steamed mussels, scrubbed and debearded, any unopened shells discarded ✦ 3 scallions, minced ✦ ½ pound precooked cocktail shrimp ✦ ½ pound silken tofu, cut into ½-inch cubes ✦ ½ cup seaweed salad ✦ ½ cup shredded carrots ✦ ½ cup softened wakame (dried seaweed) ✦ 2 tablespoons shredded daikon (Japanese radish) ✦ 2 teaspoons grated fresh horseradish ✦ 1 teaspoon soy sauce

Knishes {MAKES 4 LARGE KNISHES}

A knish is a baked, savory potato dumpling. Call it a Jewish empanada. Knisheries once dotted Manhattan's Lower East Side. Today, there's just one store left: Yonah Schimmel's. Ours is a tribute to theirs, far superior to the gummy, greasy substitutes now sold in Midtown. It's as traditional as it comes: full of mashed potatoes and broccoli, flavored with onions fried in schmaltz—or margarine, for the faint of heart. Schmaltz is rendered chicken fat, used like butter in some Jewish households. It can be bought at kosher butchers or in the meat section of some supermarkets.

For the filling
2 pounds medium baking potatoes, such as Russets, scrubbed
4 cups broccoli florets
½ cup schmaltz or margarine
1 small onion, finely chopped
2 teaspoons salt, or to taste
1 teaspoon freshly ground black pepper

For the dough
2 large egg whites, lightly beaten, at room temperature
2 tablespoons canola or other vegetable oil, plus additional for the baking sheet
½ teaspoon salt
¾ cup water
3 cups or more all-purpose flour, plus additional for dusting

1. To make the filling, bring a large pot of salted water to a boil. Add the potatoes and cook until they are soft when pierced with a fork, about 30 minutes. Drain and cool just until you can handle them. Slip the skins off with your fingers or a paring knife, then press them through a potato ricer into a large bowl. Cool completely.

2. Meanwhile, steam the broccoli florets for 4 minutes in a vegetable steamer placed over a small amount of boiling salted water. Cool, then finely chop the broccoli.

3. Melt the schmaltz or margarine in a small skillet over very low heat. Add the onion and cook until golden, about 15 minutes, stirring often. If the onion begins to brown, remove the pan from the heat for a minute, lower the heat even further, then continue cooking, stirring frequently.

4. Mix the fried onion and chopped broccoli into the riced potatoes with a wooden spoon. Season with salt and pepper; set aside.

5. To make the dough, whisk the egg whites, oil, and salt together in a large bowl. Whisk in the water, then the flour, just until a dough forms. Turn the dough out onto a lightly floured work surface and knead for 10 minutes, pulling it with one hand while pressing into it with the palm of the other. You may need to add a little extra flour if the dough is too sticky. Once the dough is smooth, cover it with a clean kitchen towel and let rest for 15 minutes.

6. Position the rack in the center of the oven and preheat the oven to 350°F. Lightly oil a large baking sheet or line it with a silicon baking mat.

7. Divide the dough into quarters. Lay one quarter on a lightly floured work surface and roll it into a 12-inch circle with a floured rolling pin. Mound a quarter of the filling into the circle's center, then fold up the sides to meet on the top. Cut off any excess dough and crimp the edges of the remaining dough together, making a crinkly, tent-like top to the knish. Warning: don't make the dough too tight around the filling, since it expands somewhat as it bakes. If the dough is not tacky enough to stick to itself, brush it with a little water to make it stick. Place the knish on the prepared baking sheet and repeat with the remaining dough and filling, creating four knishes.

8. Bake for 40 minutes, or until golden. Cool for 5 minutes on a wire rack, then serve.

Cheese Knishes Reduce the broccoli to 2 cups. Add 2 cups grated Cheddar, Asiago, or blue cheese to the potato mixture.

Chicken Liver Knishes Reduce the broccoli to 2 cups. Add ½ pound chicken livers to the skillet with the onions. Cook for 5 more minutes. Chop the chicken livers before adding them to the potato mixture.

Meat Knishes Reduce the broccoli to 2 cups. Fry ½ pound lean ground beef with the onions until the beef is brown, about 10 minutes. Stir into the potato mixture.

Mushroom Knishes Omit the broccoli. Sauté 1½ pounds button mushrooms, cleaned and thinly sliced, in the schmaltz or margarine until they give off their liquid and it evaporates. Cool the mushrooms, then chop them and add to the potato mixture.

Lasagna

In this version of an American favorite, sliced potatoes replace the wide, flat noodles. The potatoes bake up just a little crunchy in the rich tomato sauce—the creamy cheese filling beautifully complements them. Freeze portions of this casserole for dinners later in the month. This nontraditional lasagna is also great for anyone suffering from wheat allergies.

For the potato layers
2 pounds baking potatoes, such as Russets, scrubbed

For the sauce
1 tablespoon olive oil
1 large onion, finely chopped
2 garlic cloves, minced
1 pound lean ground beef
1 tablespoon minced fresh oregano
1 tablespoon minced fresh basil
1 teaspoon fennel seeds
1 teaspoon salt
1/2 teaspoon freshly ground black pepper
1/4 teaspoon crushed red pepper flakes
One 28-ounce can diced tomatoes, or whole tomatoes, diced, their juice reserved
One 6-ounce can tomato paste

For the cheese filling
1 pound ricotta (regular, low-fat, or fat-free)
2 cups shredded mozzarella (regular, low-fat, or fat-free—about 8 ounces)
1/4 cup chopped fresh parsley
1/2 teaspoon grated nutmeg
2 large eggs, at room temperature

For the casserole
1 teaspoon olive oil
1/2 cup grated Parmigiano-Reggiano (about 2 ounces)

1. To make the potato "noodles," peel the potatoes. Fit the food processor with the 1-millimeter slicing blade; slice the potatoes, emptying the bowl as necessary. You may also use a mandoline or even a large, sturdy vegetable peeler, although with this latter tool, you must be sure to make the thinnest but widest slices possible. Place all the slices in a large bowl, cover them with water, and set aside.

2. To make the sauce, heat a large skillet or sauté pan over medium heat. Swirl in the oil, then add the onion and cook until soft and fragrant, about 3 minutes, stirring frequently. Add the garlic and cook for 30 seconds. Stir in the ground beef with a wooden spoon and cook only until it has lost its raw, pink color, about a minute, stirring constantly. Stir in the oregano, basil, fennel seeds, salt, black pepper, and red pepper flakes; cook just until the spices are redolent, about 30 seconds. Pour in the tomatoes with their juice and stir in the tomato paste. Simmer, partially covered, until slightly thickened, about 15 minutes, stirring often. Set aside.

3. To make the cheese filling, stir the ricotta, mozzarella, parsley, and nutmeg in a large bowl with a wooden spoon until well combined. Stir in the eggs until creamy and uniform. Set aside. (The dish can be prepared up to this point ahead of time. Cover the potato slices in water, put the sauce and cheese filling in separate containers, and refrigerate for up to two days. Bring the ingredients back to room temperature before proceeding.)

4. Set 1 cup prepared tomato sauce aside in a small bowl for the top of the lasagna. To assemble the lasagna, position the rack in the center of the oven and preheat the oven to 350°F. Pour the olive oil into a 9 × 13-inch baking pan and grease the pan, using a piece of wax paper or a paper towel. Spread ¼ cup tomato sauce over the bottom of the pan.

5. Remove one third of the potato slices from the water and blot them dry with paper towels. Lay them over the tomato sauce in the pan, overlapping as necessary to create a seamless layer. Carefully spoon half the cheese mixture into the pan in small dollops. Use a moistened rubber spatula to spread these as evenly as possible. Be careful—the potato slices can slip around.

6. Spoon half the remaining tomato mixture over the cheese; spread it evenly across the pan. Remove half the remaining potato slices from the water and blot these dry with paper towels. Create a second layer of potato slices, top with the remaining cheese mixture, then with the other half of the tomato mixture.

7. Blot the last of the potato slices dry and use them to create a top layer for the lasagna. Spread the reserved tomato sauce over them, then sprinkle the grated Parmigiano-Reggiano evenly over the dish. Cover the pan loosely with foil and bake for 40 minutes.

8. Uncover and bake for an additional 20 minutes, or until the cheese and tomatoes are bubbling. Let stand for 5 minutes, then serve immediately. The baked casserole can be also be frozen—once it has cooled completely, cover it tightly with foil, or cut it into 8 individual portions, each wrapped tightly in wax paper, then foil. Freeze for up to two months; bring back to room temperature before reheating, either covered in a 350°F oven for 20 minutes, or uncovered for 4 minutes in a microwave set on high.

Crab and Potato Lasagna Omit the ground beef. Spread ½ pound lump crabmeat, picked over for shell and cartilage, over the first cheese layer; spread a second ½ pound lump crabmeat over the second layer.

Mushroom and Potato Lasagna Add ½ pound button mushrooms, cleaned and thinly sliced, to the tomato sauce with the ground beef.

Shrimp and Potato Lasagna Omit the ground beef. Place ½ pound medium shrimp, peeled and deveined, over the first cheese layer; then place a second ½ pound medium shrimp, peeled and deveined, over the second cheese layer.

Spicy Potato Lasagna Omit the ground beef; add 1 pound chorizo sausage, cut into 1-inch sections, to the tomato sauce before you add the spices.

Vegetarian Potato Lasagna Omit the ground beef. Add 1 pound mushrooms, cleaned and thinly sliced, to the tomato sauce before you add the spices. Lay 8 asparagus spears on top of the first cheese layer; sprinkle 1 cup peas over the second layer.

Latkes with a Quick Applesauce

{MAKES ABOUT 24 POTATO PANCAKES}

These fried potato pancakes are traditional at Hanukkah, the Jewish festival of light. Folklore claims that the oil in the skillet reminds us of the oil lamps that miraculously burned for eight days. But you don't need any theological justification to make these crisp, light potato pancakes. Traditionally, latkes are served with sour cream and applesauce.

5 pounds yellow-fleshed potatoes, preferably Yukon Golds, scrubbed
1 large onion
1 large egg, at room temperature, beaten until frothy
1 tablespoon salt, or to taste
1 tablespoon freshly ground black pepper
1½ cups canola or other vegetable oil
3 cups Quick Applesauce (recipe follows), or purchased applesauce, for garnish
1 cup sour cream or yogurt (regular, low-fat, or fat-free), for garnish

1. Peel the potatoes. Using a potato grater or the small holes of a box grater, grate the potatoes into a large fine-mesh sieve or a colander lined with cheesecloth. Set over a large bowl and drain for 10 minutes. Lightly press the potatoes with your hands or the back of a wooden spoon to get rid of any excess moisture. Discard the liquid.

2. Grate the onion into a large bowl, using either a potato grater or the small holes of a box grater. Mix in the drained potatoes with a wooden spoon. Stir in the egg, salt, and pepper until well combined.

3. Place a large high-sided skillet or sauté pan over medium heat. Pour in the oil and heat until it ripples. Scoop out ¼ cup of the potato mixture, slip it into the oil, and flatten gently with the back of a wooden spoon to create a pancake. Repeat, creating four or five latkes in the pan. Fry for 2 minutes, turn with a spatula, then fry for 2 more minutes, or until golden. Transfer the latkes to a plate lined with paper towels to drain. Repeat with the remaining potato mixture. As you continue frying the latkes, more liquid may leach out of the potato mixture in the bowl. Avoid using the wet part of the mixture—it sometimes helps to tip the bowl slightly, resting it on a piece of cardboard or the handle of a knife. As you get to the bottom of the batter, squeeze out any excess moisture with your hands before using the potato mixture for frying.

4. Serve the latkes warm with applesauce and dollops of sour cream or yogurt for garnish.

Quick Applesauce   {MAKES ABOUT 3 CUPS}

> 5 McIntosh, Macoun, or Cortland apples, peeled, cored, and chopped
> 1/2 cup water
> 1/4 cup sugar
> 1/2 teaspoon salt

Combine the apples, water, sugar, and salt in a medium pot set over medium heat. Cook, stirring often, until the apples are bubbling and begin to break apart, about 5 minutes. Reduce the heat to low. Cook for 5 more minutes, stirring often and mashing the apples with the back of a wooden spoon. The sauce should have a smooth, creamy texture. Serve warm or at room temperature. Store covered in the refrigerator for up to four days.

Leek Soup {MAKES 4 SERVINGS}

Nothing could be easier—or more satisfying—than this Welsh soup. With crunchy bread and a simple salad of berries tossed with balsamic vinegar, it's a comforting meal any time. To keep the potatoes from browning, peel and cut them just before you add them to the broth—peeling them ahead of time and covering them with water makes the soup too runny.

1 tablespoon unsalted butter, at room temperature
1/2 pound slab bacon, or thick-cut bacon, cut into 1/2-inch pieces
4 large leeks, white and pale green parts only, cut in half, well rinsed, and thinly sliced
6 cups (1 1/2 quarts) chicken stock
2 pounds yellow-fleshed potatoes, such as Yukon Golds or Charlottes, scrubbed
1/2 teaspoon freshly ground black pepper
Salt to taste (optional)

1. Melt the butter in a large pot set over medium heat. Add the bacon and cook until crispy, about 3 minutes, stirring occasionally. Add the leeks and cook until soft, about 7 minutes, stirring occasionally. Stir in the chicken stock.

2. Peel the potatoes and cut them into 1-inch chunks; add them to the soup the moment they're cut. Cover the pot and simmer over low heat until the potatoes are soft when pierced with a fork, about 15 minutes. Stir occasionally to keep the soup from sticking.

3. Transfer 2 cups of the soup to a blender or food processor fitted with the chopping blade. Puree this mixture, then whisk it back into the soup. Cook for 2 minutes, to heat through; stir in the pepper, and salt, if desired. Serve immediately.

French Leek and Potato Soup Replace the bacon with pancetta. Stir 1 tablespoon chopped tarragon and 1 teaspoon cider vinegar into the soup with the potatoes.

Herbed Leek and Potato Soup Stir 1 tablespoon chopped fresh rosemary and 2 teaspoons fresh thyme into the soup with the potatoes.

Leek and Potato Blue Cheese Soup Stir 1 cup crumbled blue cheese (about 4 ounces) into the soup after whisking in the puree.

Leek and Potato Cheese Soup Stir 1½ cups shredded Gruyère (about 6 ounces) into the soup after whisking in the puree.

Leek, Potato, and Beet Soup Reduce the potatoes to 1½ pounds. Add ½ pound golden beets, peeled and cut into 1-inch pieces, with the remaining potatoes.

Leek, Potato, and Carrot Soup Reduce the potatoes to 1½ pounds. Add ½ pound peeled and thinly sliced carrots to the soup with the remaining potatoes.

Leek, Potato, and Parsnip Soup Reduce the potatoes to 1 pound. Add 1 pound peeled and thinly sliced parsnips to the soup with the remaining potatoes.

Leek, Potato, and Turnip Soup Reduce the potatoes to 1½ pounds. Add ½ pound peeled and diced turnips to the soup with the remaining potatoes.

Ma'afe {MAKES 6 SERVINGS}

On festival days, the Bambara people of Mali make a soothing potato stew thickened with peanuts. Its earthiness is said to set the world aright again, to heal a dislocation caused by the living and the dead losing touch. The base recipe is vegetarian; the variations add meat. Make sure you buy unsalted roasted peanuts for this dish.

1½ cups unsalted roasted peanuts

2 cups water

2 tablespoons canola or other vegetable oil

1 medium onion, coarsely chopped

1 medium red bell pepper, cored, seeded, and diced

3 garlic cloves, minced

2 teaspoons salt, or to taste

½ teaspoon ground cayenne pepper, or to taste

4 Roma tomatoes (about ½ pound), diced

2 pounds sweet potatoes, such as Jewels or Red Garnets, scrubbed, peeled, and cut into 1-inch cubes

1 pound red-skinned potatoes, preferably fingerlings such as Ruby Crescents or Russian Bananas, scrubbed, then halved, or cut into 1-inch pieces if over 3 inches long

1 pound red chard, stems removed, washed for sand, and shredded

1. Pulse the peanuts in a food processor just until chopped, not smooth. Add the water and pulse until a chunky peanut butter is formed. Set aside.

2. Heat a large pot or Dutch oven over medium heat. Swirl in the oil, then add the onion and bell pepper. Cook until soft and fragrant, about 4 minutes. Add the garlic and cook for 30 seconds. Add the salt and cayenne; cook for 20 seconds, stirring constantly. Be careful—the volatilized cayenne oils can burn your eyes.

3. Stir in the tomatoes and cook until bubbly, about 3 minutes, stirring frequently. Add the sweet potatoes and fingerlings, then the reserved peanut sauce. (If the peanut sauce has broken—that is, if the oil has separated from the peanuts—pulse several times in the food processor to reincorporate.) Stir the peanut sauce until it thoroughly coats the vegetables, then add just enough water to cover them, about 3 cups, possibly more. Bring the stew to a boil, reduce the heat to low, and simmer, covered, until the potatoes are soft when pierced with a fork, about 15 minutes.

4. Stir in the red chard. Cook, uncovered, for 5 minutes, stirring frequently, until the chard has wilted and the stew is very fragrant. Check to see if it needs more salt, then serve immediately. (This stew freezes well for up to three months, either in individual containers to be thawed and reheated in the microwave or in a large freezer-safe bag.)

Caribbean Ma'afe Omit the sweet potatoes. Add 1 pound turnips, peeled and cut into 1-inch cubes, and 2 plantains, cut into 1-inch sections, with the remaining potatoes.

Chicken Ma'afe Brown 1 pound chicken breasts, cut into 1-inch cubes, in the oil before adding the tomatoes.

Lamb Ma'afe Brown 1 pound lamb, cut into 1-inch cubes, in the oil before adding the tomatoes.

Mild Ma'afe Omit the cayenne. Stir in 1 cup shredded arugula leaves, stemmed and washed, with the chard.

Manhattan Clam Chowder

{MAKES 4 SERVINGS}

Here's a hearty tomato-based stew, sure to chase away the winter doldrums, but light enough for a spring evening. Have lots of bread on hand to sop up every drop.

3 tablespoons unsalted butter, at room temperature

1 large onion, chopped

2 celery stalks, thinly sliced

1 small green bell pepper, cored, seeded, and diced

1½ pounds yellow-fleshed potatoes, such as Yukon Golds, Rattes, or Charlottes, scrubbed and cut into ½-inch pieces

One 15-ounce can diced tomatoes, or whole tomatoes, cut up, their juice reserved

2 cups fish stock, bottled clam juice, or chicken stock

Two 6½-ounce cans chopped clams, drained, liquid reserved

2 teaspoons fresh thyme

2 teaspoons chopped fresh oregano

½ teaspoon crushed red pepper flakes

3 tablespoons chopped fresh parsley

½ teaspoon salt

1. Melt the butter in a large saucepan over medium heat. Add the onion, celery, and pepper; cook until soft, about 4 minutes, stirring occasionally. Stir in the potatoes, then add the tomatoes, stock, and the liquid reserved from the drained clams. Bring the mixture to a boil over high heat. Reduce the heat to medium-low, cover, and simmer until the potatoes are tender when pierced with a fork, about 7 minutes.

2. Stir in the drained clams, thyme, oregano, and crushed red pepper flakes. Simmer, uncovered, for 5 minutes, stirring occasionally. Stir in the parsley and salt; serve immediately.

Double Clam Chowder Increase the stock to 3 cups. Add ½ pound small clams, such as littlenecks or Pismos, scrubbed, with the canned clams. Simmer for 7 minutes, or until the clams open. Discard any clams that do not open.

Manhattan Clam and Fennel Chowder Reduce the potatoes to 1 pound. Trim and thinly slice a small fennel bulb; sauté with the potatoes.

Manhattan Clam and Vegetable Chowder Increase the stock to 3 cups. Add one 10-ounce package frozen peas, thawed, or mixed frozen vegetables, thawed, with the clams.

Manhattan Fish and Clam Chowder Increase the stock to 3 cups. Add ½ pound skinless, cubed white fish fillets (such as cod, flounder, halibut, or turbot) with the clams and spices.

Southwestern Clam Chowder Omit the thyme, oregano, and parsley. Add 1 cup corn kernels (if fresh, about 1 large ear, or frozen corn, thawed), 1 tablespoon chili powder, 1 teaspoon ground cumin, and ¼ teaspoon grated nutmeg with the clams. Stir in 3 tablespoons chopped cilantro with the salt.

Spicy Manhattan Clam Chowder Reduce the stock to 1½ cups. Add ½ cup red wine with the stock. Increase the crushed red pepper flakes to 1 teaspoon and add ¼ teaspoon ground cinnamon with the spices.

Masala Dosa {MAKES 4 SERVINGS}

This Indian dish wraps a fragrant, savory stuffing (masala) in a light, low-fat crepe made from rice flour (dosa). Serve this hearty, spicy dinner either by offering the filling and crepes separately and allowing your guests to build their own masala dosa, or by stuffing the crepes yourself, rolling them up, and topping them with diced tomatoes and cucumbers and dollops of yogurt. If you don't want to make the dosa, purchase lefse or lavash—both are thin, white, tortilla-like breads.

Rice flour is a powdery flour made from white rice. It's used primarily for baked goods. It's usually available in Asian markets, Indian markets, and most gourmet supermarkets, as well as from outlets listed in the Source Guide (page 251). Do not confuse rice flour with "glutinous rice flour," made from glutinous rice, which creates a very sticky dough and is used for candies and desserts.

For the masala

1½ pounds large red-skinned potatoes, such as Red Clouds, Red Golds, or
  Desirées, scrubbed
3 tablespoons canola or other vegetable oil
1½ teaspoons mustard seeds
1 teaspoon cumin seeds
6 fresh basil leaves
2 large onions, thinly sliced
1 tablespoon minced fresh ginger
1 serrano chile, seeded and chopped
½ teaspoon turmeric
½ teaspoon salt, or to taste
¼ teaspoon ground cayenne pepper, or to taste
1¼ cups vegetable stock, or more as needed
1 teaspoon fresh lime juice

1. Bring a medium pot of salted water to a boil. Add the potatoes and cook until still firm when pierced with a fork, about 12 minutes. Drain and cool until you can handle them. Slip off the peels with your hands or a sharp paring knife; cut into ½-inch dice. Set aside.

2. Heat a large skillet or sauté pan over medium heat. Swirl in the oil, then add the mustard and cumin seeds. Cook for 20 seconds, stirring constantly; add the basil leaves and cook for 10 seconds. Add the onions, reduce the heat to very low, and cook until golden, about 15 minutes, stirring frequently and lowering the heat even more if the onions begin to brown.

3. Stir in the ginger, chile, turmeric, salt, and cayenne; cook for 1 minute, stirring constantly. Add the potatoes and 1 cup of the stock; cover and cook over low heat, stirring occasionally, for 5 minutes. Add ¼ cup more of the stock, cover, and cook another 5 minutes, or until the potatoes start to break apart. If the stew dries out, add more stock in ¼-cup increments as needed. Stir in the lime juice; season with salt, if desired; and serve immediately with dosa (recipe follows).

Dosa

> 1 cup all-purpose flour
> 1 cup rice flour
> ½ teaspoon salt
> 2 cups water
> 1 cup yogurt (regular or low-fat, but not fat-free)
>
> Vegetable oil spray for the skillet

1. Place the all-purpose flour, the rice flour, and salt in a food processor or a blender; pulse until well combined. Add the water and yogurt; pulse until a wet batter is formed.

2. Coat a medium skillet (preferably nonstick) lightly with vegetable oil spray, then heat over medium heat. Pour ⅓ cup batter into the skillet, quickly swirling it around to spread the batter evenly across the pan. Cook for 1 or 2 minutes, just until the crepe begins to bubble and brown. Flip the crepe, using a spatula safe for nonstick surfaces. Cook for 1 minute, until the crepe browns and begins to bubble up from the inside. Remove from the pan and repeat with the remaining batter. The dosa can be kept warm in a 250°F oven for no more than 10 minutes. Spray the pan again after every three or four crepes as needed to prevent them from sticking. Serve with the masala filling.

Meat Loaf

This variation on Mom's classic is stuffed with shredded potatoes and melted mango chutney. There are two schools of thought on the meat loaf: a loaf in a bread pan or a mound on a baking sheet. We affectionately refer to the latter as "meat lump"—although it is our preference. It gets crisp on the outside without steaming and turning into a meat pudding as do those baked in pans.

For the filling

1½ pounds baking potatoes, such as Russets, scrubbed

2 tablespoons canola or other vegetable oil

¼ cup mango chutney

¼ cup chopped fresh cilantro

2 teaspoons salt, or to taste

½ teaspoon freshly ground black pepper

For the meat loaf

1 pound lean ground beef

½ pound ground veal (see Note)

½ pound ground pork

2 tablespoons dehydrated minced onion

2 tablespoons ketchup

2 tablespoons Dijon mustard

1 large egg, at room temperature

¼ cup plain dried bread crumbs

2 teaspoons salt, or to taste

1 teaspoon fresh thyme

½ teaspoon ground cumin

½ teaspoon ground cinnamon

½ teaspoon freshly ground black pepper

1. Position the rack in the center of the oven and preheat the oven to 350°F. To make the filling, peel the potatoes, then shred them using the large holes of a box grater or a food processor fitted with the shredding blade.

Working in small batches, squeeze the shredded potatoes over the sink to get rid of any excess water, then place them in a large bowl.

2. Heat a medium skillet over medium heat. Swirl in the oil, then add the shredded potatoes and cook until softened, about 5 minutes, stirring constantly. Transfer them back to the bowl and stir in the chutney, cilantro, salt, and pepper. Set aside.

3. To make the meat loaf, place the ground beef, ground veal, and ground pork in a large bowl. Mix together with your hands, working gently so as not to destroy the meat's fibers. Add the dehydrated onion, ketchup, mustard, egg, bread crumbs, salt, thyme, cumin, cinnamon, and pepper; continue mixing by hand just until uniform (but not smooth).

4. In either a 10-cup oval roasting pan or a 9 × 13-inch pan, press one third of the mixture into a flat oval about 6 × 10 inches. Mound the potato filling into the middle of the meat oval, leaving a ½-inch border all the way around.

5. Place the remaining meat mixture between two sheets of wax paper. Roll it or flatten it to a larger oval, about 8 × 12 inches. Peel off the top sheet of wax paper, then gently place the flattened meat on top of the filling. Peel off the second sheet of wax paper, then mold the top layer around the filling and gently press down to the bottom oval. Seal the loaf by pinching the meat together, then smoothing it closed.

6. Bake the meat loaf for 1 hour, or until it is golden brown. Cool for 5 minutes, then serve.

NOTE *If you can't find ground veal, simply use 1½ pounds ground beef.*

Cabbage-Stuffed Meat Loaf Decrease the potatoes to ¾ pound. Blanch 2 cups thinly sliced napa cabbage in boiling water for 2 minutes, then drain it thoroughly, squeeze out any excess water, and add it to the filling.

Carrot-Stuffed Meat Loaf Decrease the potatoes to 1 pound. Shred 4 large carrots along with the remaining potatoes and add them to the filling.

Cranberry Meat Loaf Decrease the potatoes to 1¼ pounds and omit the cilantro and chutney. Add ¼ cup canned whole cranberry sauce, ¼ cup dried cranberries, ¼ cup chopped toasted pecans, and 2 tablespoons chopped fresh sage to the filling. Omit the cumin from the meat mixture.

Pickled Meat Loaf Omit the mango chutney and stir ¼ cup pickle relish into the filling.

Raisin- and Nut-Stuffed Meat Loaf Reduce the potatoes to 1¼ pounds. Add ½ cup raisins or dried currants and ¼ cup chopped toasted walnuts to the filling.

Sweet-and-Sour Meat Loaf Omit the mango chutney. Stir ¼ cup blueberry jam, 2 tablespoons cider vinegar, and 4 or more dashes Tabasco sauce into the filling.

Moussaka {MAKES 6 SERVINGS}

Originally a simple Greek casserole of seasoned ground lamb layered with slices of eggplant, moussaka is now a favorite across the Middle East, where there are many variations. This American version is assembled by a technique inspired by Craig Claiborne in his *New York Times Cookbook*. But he never considered what potatoes would do for the dish—undoubtedly the only oversight in an otherwise splendid career.

3 large eggplants
½ cup olive oil, plus additional for oiling the pan and the
    aluminum foil
1 medium onion, minced
2 garlic cloves, minced
½ pound ground lamb
½ cup sweet vermouth or port
2 teaspoons ground cinnamon
2 teaspoons salt, or to taste
1 teaspoon ground cumin
1 teaspoon freshly ground black pepper
1½ pounds baking potatoes, preferably Russets, scrubbed
2 large eggs, at room temperature, lightly beaten

1. Cut the eggplant in half, then score the cut side with a sharp paring knife without breaking the skin at the edges. Heat a large skillet over high heat. Swirl in 2 tablespoons of the oil, then add two eggplant halves, cut side down. Sear for 1 minute without disturbing, then add 3 tablespoons water. Cover and reduce the heat to low. Steam the eggplant halves for 10 minutes. Set the halves aside to cool on a large platter and repeat with the remaining halves.

2. After the eggplant has cooled enough that you can handle it, scrape the pulp into a large bowl using a teaspoon, taking care not to break the skin. You should have 4 cups eggplant pulp. Reserve the skins, discarding any additional pulp.

3. Heat a large skillet or sauté pan over medium heat. Swirl in the remaining 2 tablespoons oil, then add the onion and cook until soft and fragrant, about 2 minutes, stirring frequently. Stir in the garlic; cook for 30 seconds. Add the ground lamb and cook until lightly browned, about 2 minutes, stirring constantly.

4. Add the reserved 4 cups eggplant pulp and the sweet vermouth; mix well with a wooden spoon, then stir in the cinnamon, salt, cumin, and pepper. Continue cooking until the eggplant gives off its liquid and begins to coat the pan with a fine film, about 5 minutes, stirring constantly. Set aside to cool for at least 30 minutes. (The eggplant filling can be made up to this point a day in advance; cover tightly when cooled and refrigerate, then allow to come back to room temperature before proceeding.)

5. Peel the potatoes and cut them in half. Beginning with the cut side, cut off thin slices, using a sharp knife or a sturdy vegetable peeler. (You don't want paper-thin slices; make them about the thickness of lasagna noodles.) Place the potato slices in a large bowl of water as you work.

6. Bring a medium pot of salted water to a boil. Drain the potato slices and add them to the pot. Cook just until crisp, about 3 minutes. Drain—be careful, for they are fragile—and set aside.

7. Mix the eggs into the eggplant pulp mixture. Position the rack in the center of the oven and preheat the oven to 350°F. Oil a 2-quart high-sided soufflé dish with olive oil.

8. Place the eggplant skins in the soufflé dish, skin side out, so that they meet and overlap on the bottom, then rise up along the insides of the dish. In other words, the eggplant skins should form a kind of "skin" around the moussaka as it bakes. Overlap them as necessary. If any tear, plug the hole with a small amount of the eggplant pulp mixture. Let the skins hang over the top of the soufflé dish.

9. Lay one fifth of the potato slices on top of the eggplant skins on the bottom of the dish. Top with 1 cup eggplant pulp mixture. Build three more layers, then top with a final layer of potato slices. Fold the eggplant skins over to seal the dish. If the skins don't meet, it doesn't matter.

10. Oil a 10-inch-long piece of foil. Place it, oiled side down, over the casserole and loosely seal it. Bake the moussaka for 1 hour 30 minutes. Cool on a wire rack for 10 minutes, then serve.

Cheesy Potato Moussaka Layer 2 tablespoons grated Manchego or other sheep's milk cheese on top of each layer of potatoes (you'll need ½ cup plus 2 tablespoons, or about 3 ounces).

Lebanese Moussaka Stir ½ cup raisins and ½ cup slivered almonds into the eggplant mixture. Each layer of eggplant pulp mixture in the casserole will be 1¼ cups, rather than 1 cup.

Vegetarian Moussaka Omit the ground lamb. Stir 2 cups cooked kasha into the eggplant pulp mixture.

Mushroom Stew

Unlike the smooth Curried Mushroom Soup (page 68), this one, laced with diced potatoes, tastes both lighter and chunkier. The stew tastes even better the day after it's made, but you'll need to thin it out with more stock as you reheat it, because the potatoes give off starch and absorb liquid as they sit.

3 tablespoons olive oil

2 medium onions, chopped

3 garlic cloves, minced

1 pound cremini mushrooms, cleaned and roughly chopped

1 pound shiitake mushrooms, stemmed, cleaned, and caps roughly chopped

½ pound red-skinned potatoes, such as Red Blisses or All Reds, cut into ½-inch pieces

½ pound yellow-fleshed potatoes, such as Austrian Crescents or Yukon Golds, cut into ½-inch pieces

1 tablespoon minced fresh rosemary

1 tablespoon minced fresh sage

1 tablespoon fresh thyme

2 cups mushroom or vegetable stock

½ cup chopped fresh parsley

1 teaspoon salt

½ teaspoon freshly ground black pepper

1. Heat a large pot over medium-high heat. Swirl in the oil, then add the onions and cook until soft and fragrant, about 4 minutes, stirring often. Add the garlic and cook for 30 seconds. Stir in the cremini and shiitake mushrooms; cook just until the mushrooms begin to give off their liquid, about 3 minutes, stirring frequently.

2. Stir in both kinds of potatoes with a wooden spoon, then add the rosemary, sage, and thyme. Cook just until aromatic, about 30 seconds. Stir in the stock, cover, and reduce the heat to low. Simmer until the potatoes are soft when pierced with a fork, about 12 minutes. Gently stir in the parsley, salt, and pepper and cook for another 2 minutes to bind the flavors. Serve immediately. The soup can be made in advance—store it covered in the refrigerator for up to three days, but thin it out with extra stock as you reheat it.

The stew can be varied with a seemingly limitless list of mushrooms. Substitute hedgehog, lobster, black trumpet, porcini, portobello, or hen of the woods, so long as you have a total of 2 pounds.

You can also finish the stew with one of several enhancers. Along with the parsley, stir in one of the following:
2 tablespoons dry vermouth ✦ 1½ tablespoons sweet vermouth ✦ 1½ tablespoons Chinese black vinegar ✦ 1 tablespoon basil oil ✦ 2 teaspoons sesame oil ✦ 4 dashes Tabasco sauce, or to taste

New England Clam Chowder

{MAKES 6 SERVINGS}

New England clam chowder is often thickened with flour, which can cause the soup to morph into a gloppy mess. This version solves that problem by using more potatoes than most, giving the soup body and depth. The extra potato starch also means less cream, which makes the soup healthier, as well as better tasting. Store it covered in the refrigerator for up to three days.

1 teaspoon canola or other vegetable oil

4 slices bacon, finely chopped

1 large onion, finely chopped

2 celery stalks, thinly sliced

1 garlic clove, minced

1½ pounds red-skinned potatoes, such as Red Blisses, or even fingerlings like
    Ruby Crescents, scrubbed and cut into ½-inch pieces

Two 6½-ounce cans clams, drained, their liquid reserved

1½ cups fish, vegetable, or chicken stock

2 cups milk, or more as necessary (regular or low-fat, but not fat-free)

½ cup heavy cream

3 tablespoons chopped fresh parsley

½ teaspoon salt

½ teaspoon freshly ground pepper, preferably white

¼ teaspoon grated nutmeg

1. Heat a large pot or a Dutch oven over medium heat. Swirl in the oil, then add the bacon and fry until crisp, about 4 minutes, stirring frequently. Remove the bacon with a slotted spoon; set aside on a plate lined with paper towels to drain.

2. Add the onion to the bacon drippings; cook until soft and translucent, about 3 minutes, stirring often. Add the celery and garlic and cook for 30 seconds; then stir in the potatoes, the liquid reserved from the drained clams, the stock, and milk. Bring to a boil, reduce the heat to low, and cook, uncovered, until the potatoes are tender when pierced with a fork, about 7 minutes, stirring occasionally. If too much liquid evaporates while the potatoes are cooking, reduce the heat further and add more milk in ¼-cup increments as necessary.

3. When the potatoes are tender, stir in the reserved bacon, clams, cream, parsley, salt, pepper, and nutmeg. Heat through without boiling, then serve immediately.

Clam and Chicken Chowder Brown 1 pound chicken breasts, cut into 1-inch cubes, in the rendered bacon drippings before adding the onion. Remove the chicken and set aside. Return the chicken pieces to the pot with the potatoes.

Clam and Corn Chowder Add 2 cups corn kernels (about 2 large ears, or frozen kernels, thawed) with the potatoes.

Fresh Clam Chowder Omit the canned clams. Add one 12-ounce bottle clam juice with the potatoes, stock, and milk. Add 1 pound clams, scrubbed and debearded, before adding the cream and spices. Simmer, covered, until the clams open, about 5 minutes, then add the remaining ingredients. Discard any clams that don't open.

Vegetable Chowder Omit the clams and their juice. Increase the milk to 2½ cups. Add ½ pound carrots, cut into ½-inch rounds, and ½ pound parsnips, peeled and cut into ½-inch rounds, with the potatoes.

Nikujaga

This is home-style Japanese cooking at its best: a one-pot dish, lightly seasoned with sesame oil and sake, or rice wine. The name literally means "meat and potatoes." The real secret is the broth made from bonito flakes—that is, dried mackerel shavings. Bonito flakes are available in most Asian markets and through mail order by suppliers listed in the Source Guide (page 251).

2 cups water

4 cups bonito flakes (about 1 ounce)

2 tablespoons soy sauce

1 tablespoon sesame oil

2 medium onions, halved and sliced into 1/2-inch strips

1/2 pound sirloin steak, sliced into 1/2-inch-thick strips against the grain

1 pound baking potatoes, such as Russets, scrubbed, peeled, and cut into 1-inch cubes

2 tablespoons sugar

2 tablespoons sake or dry vermouth

1. Bring the water to a boil in a medium saucepan. Stir in the bonito flakes and soy sauce, cover, and set aside to steep for 10 minutes. Strain the broth into a separate bowl, discarding the bonito flakes.

2. Heat a large skillet or sauté pan over medium heat. Swirl in the sesame oil, then add the onions. Cook until soft and fragrant, about 2 minutes, stirring frequently.

3. Add the meat; sauté just until the strips are no longer pink. Add the potatoes, then the sugar and sake, stirring with a wooden spoon until the sugar dissolves, about 20 seconds. Stir in the reserved bonito broth. Reduce the heat to low and simmer, partially covered, for 12 minutes, or until the potatoes are tender when pierced with a fork. Serve immediately.

Nikujaga and Greens Serve the stew over 1 bunch Swiss chard or mustard greens, stemmed and rinsed, then steamed 5 minutes.

Scallop Nikujaga Add ½ pound sea scallops, cut in half, after the potatoes have simmered 12 minutes.

Shrimp Nikujaga Add ½ pound medium shrimp, peeled and cleaned, after the potatoes have simmered 12 minutes.

Sweet Potato Nikujaga Omit the Russets and the sugar. Add 1 pound yams, peeled and cut into 1-inch cubes, with the sake.

Tofu-Yaga Omit the sirloin steak. Add 1 pound extra-firm tofu, cut into 1-inch cubes, to the stew after the potatoes have cooked for 10 minutes.

Noodles with Mushrooms

{MAKES 4 SERVINGS}

Popular in Dutch and German communities, potato noodles are also highly prized in farm settlements across the Midwest. Here, these supple but toothsome noodles are simply tossed with butter and sautéed mushrooms for a warm and comforting dish. Unfortunately, *potato noodles will work only with Russets.* You can double this recipe—and you might want to, since leftovers will be appreciated the next day.

½ pound medium Russet potatoes, scrubbed

1 large egg, at room temperature, beaten until frothy

1¼ teaspoons salt

2 to 3 cups all-purpose flour

4 tablespoons (½ stick) unsalted butter, at room temperature

12 ounces white button mushrooms, cleaned and thinly sliced

3 tablespoons dry vermouth or white wine

1 tablespoon chopped fresh parsley

1½ teaspoons freshly ground black pepper

1. Bring a medium pot of salted water to a boil. Meanwhile, peel the potatoes. Add them to the pot and cook until tender when pierced with a fork, about 22 minutes. Drain and cool just until they can be handled. Press them through a potato ricer into a large bowl, or gently mash them with two forks, just until they are grainy, not until smooth.

2. Stir in the egg and ¾ teaspoon of the salt with a wooden spoon, then begin stirring in the flour, ½ cup at time. Mix in enough flour to make a dough, about 2 cups in all, stirring vigorously with a wooden spoon after each ½-cup addition. The dough should be smooth but slightly sticky.

3. Turn the dough onto a floured work surface. Knead for 5 minutes by pressing into it with the heel of one hand while pulling it away with the other.

Add more flour as necessary to keep the dough from sticking, but be sparing—the dough should be slightly sticky. Cover loosely with a clean kitchen towel; set aside to rest for 5 minutes. Meanwhile, cover a large baking sheet with a second clean kitchen towel and dust the towel liberally with flour.

4. Divide the dough in half. Roll one half with a floured rolling pin on a lightly floured work surface into a rectangular sheet less than ⅛ inch thick, just a little thicker than store-bought egg noodles. Keep the work surface, the dough, and the rolling pin well floured so that the noodles don't stick. With a sharp knife or a pizza cutter, cut into noodles about ½ inch wide. Gently transfer the noodles to the prepared kitchen towel on the baking sheet. Repeat with the second half of the dough. Set the noodles aside to rest for at least 2 hours, but no more than 5 hours, before proceeding.

5. Put a large pot of salted water on to boil. Meanwhile, melt 2 tablespoons of the butter in a large skillet or sauté pan set over medium heat. Add the sliced mushrooms and cook until they give off their liquid and the liquid is reduced by half, about 7 minutes, stirring frequently. Add the vermouth; simmer for 30 seconds. Cover the pan and set aside while the noodles cook.

6. Add the noodles to the boiling water. Cook for 3 minutes, or until tender. (The water may not come back to a rolling boil.) Drain the noodles and place in a large serving bowl. Set the mushroom mixture back over low heat; stir in the remaining 2 tablespoons butter, parsley, pepper, and the remaining ½ teaspoon salt. Whisk gently until the butter melts and emulsifies into a sauce, about a minute. Pour the mushroom mixture over the noodles, toss gently, and serve immediately.

Cilantro Pesto and Potato Noodles Omit the mushroom mixture. Toss the cooked noodles with 1 cup Cilantro Pesto (page 96).

Easy Pasta Sauce Potato Noodles Omit the mushroom mixture. Toss 1½ cups jarred pasta sauce, heated through, with the cooked noodles.

Fried Onions and Potato Noodles Omit the mushroom mixture. In a large skillet, gently sauté 1 large onion, cut into ¼-inch rings, and 1 teaspoon caraway seeds, in 3 tablespoons butter over low heat for at least 30 minutes, or until the onions are golden and very sweet, stirring often. Pour these over the cooked noodles.

Potato Noodles with Sage Gorgonzola Sauce Omit the mushroom mixture. Pour Sage Gorgonzola Sauce (page 97) over the cooked noodles.

Potato Noodles with Hamburger and Mushrooms Sauté 1 pound ground beef with the mushrooms. Increase the vermouth to ¼ cup and add 1 tablespoon chopped basil and 2 teaspoons chopped oregano with it.

Potato Noodles with Roasted Red Pepper Pesto Omit the mushroom mixture. Pour Red Pepper Pesto (page 144) over the cooked noodles.

Norwegian Potato Salad

This simple salad takes no time to make but packs lots of flavor, thanks to jarred herring in cream sauce, a Norwegian staple found in the refrigerator case of most supermarkets, usually near the sour cream. The salad's even better the second day, once the flavors blend.

1¾ pounds yellow-fleshed potatoes, such as Yukon Golds or Papa Amarillas, scrubbed
2 celery stalks, finely chopped
1 small red onion, minced
2 tablespoons chopped fresh parsley
One 12-ounce jar herring fillets in sour cream or herring in cream sauce
¼ cup sour cream
½ teaspoon salt
½ teaspoon freshly ground black pepper

1. Bring a medium pot of salted water to a boil. Add the potatoes and cook until tender when pierced with a fork, about 20 minutes. Drain and cool just until you can handle them. Slip the skins off with your fingers or a sharp paring knife; cut the potatoes into ½-inch pieces. Place in a large bowl; toss with the celery, onion, and parsley.

2. In a small bowl, mix the herring, their cream sauce, the extra sour cream, salt, and pepper until well combined. Stir carefully, trying not to break up the fish. Pour over the still warm potato mixture; gently toss. Serve immediately, chill, or keep tightly covered in the refrigerator for up to four days. The salad may weep as it rests; stir to reincorporate the liquid.

An almost endless list of ingredients can be added along with the celery. Some of the best include:

¼ cup shredded carrots ✦ 1½ teaspoons minced mint ✦ 1 tablespoon chopped dill ✦ 1 tablespoon juniper berries, crushed, then cooked in the salted water with the potatoes ✦ 1 tablespoon minced fresh tarragon ✦ 1 tablespoon bottled horse-radish ✦ 2 tablespoons dry or sweet vermouth ✦ 2 tablespoons prepared mustard

Paprikash {MAKES 4 SERVINGS}

Originally a Hungarian chicken dish, veal paprikash became popular in Manhattan in the years before World War I. It was so popular, in fact, that patrons had to order it up to a week in advance just to make sure their favorite restaurant had enough on hand. Here, the noodles are replaced with potatoes. If you can't find veal shoulder meat, buy a pound and a half of veal shoulder chops, debone the meat, and cut it into chunks; or simply buy a pound of veal stew meat.

1 pound veal shoulder meat, cut into 1-inch chunks

1 teaspoon salt, or to taste

1 teaspoon freshly ground black pepper

4 tablespoons (½ stick) unsalted butter, at room temperature

2 large onions, thinly sliced

2 tablespoons sweet paprika

2 tablespoons all-purpose flour

2½ cups beef or chicken stock

1 teaspoon caraway seeds

2 pounds yellow-fleshed potatoes, such as Yukon Golds, Peanuts, or Ozettes, scrubbed

1 cup sour cream (regular, low-fat, or fat-free)

1. Position the rack in the center of the oven and preheat the oven to 350°F. Season the meat with the salt and pepper.

2. Melt 2 tablespoons of the butter in a large oven-safe sauté pan or skillet set over medium-high heat. Cook undisturbed until the butter browns, about a minute. Add the veal and cook for about 2 minutes, turning the pieces in the butter to brown them. Transfer to a platter and set aside.

3. Swirl the remaining 2 tablespoons butter into the pan. Add the onions, reduce the heat to very low, and cook until golden, about 15 minutes, stirring frequently. Add the paprika and flour; cook for 30 seconds, stirring constantly.

Pour the stock into the pan; cook until thickened, about 2 minutes, stirring constantly. Return the meat and any accumulated juices to the pan, along with the caraway seeds. Cover, place in the oven, and bake for 1 hour.

4. Meanwhile, peel the potatoes and cut them into 1-inch chunks. Place them in a large bowl and cover with water.

5. After the veal has baked for 1 hour, drain the potatoes and place them in the skillet. Stir well to coat, then bake for an additional 30 minutes, or until the potatoes are soft when pierced with a fork.

6. Remove the pan from the oven and gently stir in the sour cream, taking care not to break up the potatoes. Be careful: the pan is hot. Season with salt, if desired. Serve immediately. ·

Beer Paprikash Reduce the stock to 1 cup and add one 12-ounce bottle beer to the sauce before you add the meat. Cook, uncovered, the last 30 minutes.

Chicken Paprikash Substitute 1 pound boneless, skinless chicken breasts, cut into 1-inch chunks, for the veal.

Fiery Paprikash Substitute hot paprika, sometimes packaged as "hot Hungarian paprika," for the sweet.

Mushroom Paprikash Substitute 2 pounds cremini mushrooms, cleaned and thinly sliced, for the veal. Reduce the first baking time to 15 minutes.

Tomato Paprikash Reduce the stock to 1½ cups. Add one 15-ounce can diced tomatoes with the remaining stock.

Pasta Salad with Roasted Red Pepper Pesto {MAKES 6 SERVINGS}

Pasta and potatoes? In Rome, it's a classic, usually lightened by a bright herb pesto. This variation uses a roasted red pepper pesto and tubular pasta, which match well with the fingerling potatoes.

For the pesto
2 large red bell peppers
¼ cup pine nuts
1½ cups packed fresh parsley
½ cup extra virgin olive oil
2 garlic cloves
¼ cup grated Parmigiano-Reggiano (about 1 ounce)
1 teaspoon salt, or to taste
½ teaspoon freshly ground black pepper

For the salad
1½ pounds yellow-fleshed potatoes, preferably fingerlings such as Austrian Crescents, Peanuts, or Rattes, scrubbed
1 cup fresh peas, or frozen peas, thawed
12 ounces ziti, rigatoni, or other tubular pasta, cooked and drained according to package directions
1 large carrot, shredded

1. To make the pesto, begin by roasting the peppers. Hold them with tongs or a long-handled fork over a gas burner at high; roast until charred, about 3 minutes, turning as each side blackens. (Alternatively, roast them on a baking sheet 5 inches from a preheated broiler, turning them as they char, about 4 minutes total roasting time.) Place the blackened peppers in a paper bag or in a medium bowl tightly sealed with plastic wrap. Set aside for 15 minutes.

2. Meanwhile, position the rack in the center of the oven and preheat the oven to 350°F. Place the pine nuts on a small baking sheet and toast them for

4 minutes, stirring occasionally to keep them from burning. Remove from the oven and set aside.

3. Peel the charred peppers with your fingers—do not run water over the peppers to peel them as flavor is lost. Seed and core the peppers, then place them in a food processor fitted with the chopping blade. Add the toasted pine nuts, parsley, olive oil, garlic, cheese, salt, and pepper. Pulse seven or eight times, until smooth, scraping down the sides of the bowl if necessary. Set aside.

4. To make the salad, bring 3 quarts of salted water to a boil in a medium pot. Add the fingerlings and cook until tender when pierced with a fork, about 22 minutes. Add the peas and cook for an additional 30 seconds. Drain the pot in a colander and allow the potatoes to cool just until you can handle them. Cut them in half; or if they are longer than 3 inches, into 1-inch chunks.

5. Place the potatoes, peas, pasta, and shredded carrot in a large bowl; toss with the roasted red pepper pesto. Serve at room temperature or chilled. The salad can be kept, covered, in the refrigerator for up to three days.

Substitute ¼ cup toasted pecans, walnuts, or hazelnuts for the pine nuts. ✦ Change the vegetables in the salad. Blanch broccoli florets, cauliflower florets, green beans, or baby zucchini instead of the peas. Or add fresh sugar snaps instead of the peas. ✦ Add cooked meat to the salad, such as 2 cups cubed smoked turkey, cubed smoked ham, diced salami, or diced sopressata. ✦ Add heat to the pesto, using up to 8 dashes Tabasco sauce or up to ½ teaspoon chile oil.

Pierogi Pie {MAKES 8 SERVINGS}

This recipe doesn't make a traditional pierogi, that Polish specialty of small, half-moon pastries filled with potatoes, cabbage, and meat. To create a substantial main course, we've created a pierogi pie: one huge pierogi, baked in a springform pan and served in wedges. Make sure the eggs are at room temperature—if they're cold, they'll kill the yeast just as it begins to act.

2 pounds baking potatoes, such as Russets, scrubbed

For the dough

1 cup warm milk, between 105°F and 115°F

Two ¼-ounce packages active dry yeast

2 teaspoons sugar

2 large eggs, plus 1 large egg yolk, at room temperature, lightly beaten

1 tablespoon canola or other vegetable oil, plus additional for the bowl

½ teaspoon salt

4 cups all-purpose flour, or more as needed, plus additional for the work
  surface

For the filling

3 tablespoons unsalted butter, at room temperature

1 large red onion, chopped

1 small Savoy cabbage (about 1 pound), stemmed, cored, and chopped

1 teaspoon caraway seeds

1 cup vegetable or chicken stock

⅔ cup sour cream (regular or low-fat, but not fat-free)

2 teaspoons sugar

1 teaspoon salt, or to taste

½ teaspoon freshly ground black pepper

For the pierogi pie

Oil for the springform pan

1 large egg, beaten with 1 teaspoon water, for a wash

1. Bake the potatoes by positioning the rack in the center of the oven and preheating the oven to 400°F. Place the potatoes in the center of the rack and bake until soft, about 1 hour 15 minutes. Transfer to a cooling rack until they can be handled easily. Slip off the skins with your fingers or a sharp paring knife, then press the potatoes through a potato ricer into a large bowl; set aside. Reduce the oven temperature to 350°F.

2. To make the dough, pour the warm milk into a large bowl, then sprinkle the yeast on top. Sprinkle the sugar over the yeast, stir to dissolve, and set aside to proof, about 5 minutes, until bubbly. Stir in the eggs and egg yolk, oil, and salt with a wooden spoon until well combined; then stir in 1 cup of the flour until smooth and uniform.

3. Begin stirring in more flour, ½ cup at a time, until the dough is workable and somewhat elastic, but not smooth. (Alternatively, place the yeast mixture in the bowl of a stand mixer fitted with the dough hook. With the mixer at low, mix in the flour, ½ cup at time, until a workable—but still slightly sticky—dough is formed.)

4. If working by hand, turn the dough out onto a lightly floured work surface. Knead until elastic, about 10 minutes, pressing into it with the heel of one hand and pulling it with the fingers of the other. You may have to add more flour, in ¼-cup increments, if the dough becomes too sticky—but only add enough flour so that the dough is workable, not smooth. (If using an electric mixer, set at medium speed and knead until elastic, about 5 minutes, adding flour in ¼-cup increments if the dough sticks to the hook.)

5. Oil a large, clean bowl, then place the dough in it. Turn the dough once to coat, then cover and set aside in a warm, dry place to rise until doubled in bulk, about an hour.

6. Meanwhile, make the filling while the dough rises. Melt the butter in a large skillet or sauté pan set over medium heat. Add the onion and cook until soft and fragrant, about 4 minutes, stirring frequently. Add the cabbage and caraway seeds; cook until the cabbage is wilted, about 5 minutes, stirring constantly. Pour in the stock, mix well, and cover. Reduce the heat to low and simmer until the cabbage is tender, about 20 minutes. Cool for 10 minutes.

7. Stir the cabbage mixture into the riced potatoes, along with the sour cream, sugar, salt, and pepper. Stir just until combined, not until smooth. Lightly oil a 9-inch springform pan.

8. Turn the risen dough out onto a well-floured work surface, then roll it into a circle about 24 inches in diameter and about ⅛ inch thick with a floured rolling pin. (You may also need to flour your hands to work with this sticky dough.) Line the prepared springform pan with the dough, pressing it into the corners to conform to the pan and letting it hang over the upper lip. Spoon in the filling, pressing it down with the back of a wooden spoon. Fold the excess dough over the top, allowing it to meet in the center. (You may need to crease and buckle it to get it to fit.) Trim the dough so that it doesn't overlap too much, just so that it meets in the middle and a seam can be made. Seal to make a top crust by pinching the dough together and then smoothing it flat.

9. Brush with the egg-and-water wash, then bake for 40 minutes, or until lightly browned. Cool on a wire rack for 5 minutes, then serve.

Broccoli Pierogi Pie Substitute one 10-ounce package chopped frozen broccoli, thawed, for the cabbage.

Cheesy Pierogi Pie Stir 1 cup shredded Cheddar (about 4 ounces) into the potato mixture.

Curried Pierogi Substitute 2 teaspoons curry powder for the caraway seeds. Stir ¼ cup mango chutney into the potato mixture.

Mushroom Pierogi Pie Add ½ pound button or cremini mushrooms, cleaned and thinly sliced, with the cabbage.

Sausage Pierogi Pie Fry ½ pound sausage meat, removed from its casing, until brown in 1 teaspoon vegetable oil in a medium skillet over medium heat. Drain the meat on paper towels, then blot dry. Stir into the potato filling mixture.

Pork and Potato Stir-Fry

{MAKES 4 SERVINGS}

Potato dishes may not be traditional fare in American-Chinese restaurants, but they're now prevalent in China's eastern provinces because of the spud's growing importance in Chinese cuisine. In this dish, the potatoes are boiled for just a few minutes and are still crunchy—in keeping with the current Chinese potato-stir-frying tastes. The dish comes together very quickly, so have all the ingredients laid out before you start cooking. Both hot and sweet bean paste are condiments, or "sauce makers," usually (as here) stirred into a dish just before you're ready to serve it. You can find them both in Asian markets and some gourmet food stores—or check the Source Guide (page 251).

1½ pounds small red-skinned potatoes, such as Red Bliss or All Reds, or red-skinned fingerlings, such as Ruby Crescents, scrubbed

1 pound pork loin, trimmed of excess fat

2 tablespoons peanut oil

2 scallions, minced

2 garlic cloves, minced

3 tablespoons minced fresh ginger

2 tablespoons hot bean paste (sometimes sold as "hot bean sauce")

1 tablespoon sweet bean paste (sometimes sold as "sweet bean sauce")

2 tablespoons mirin

2 tablespoons Chinese black vinegar or 1 tablespoon Worcestershire sauce

1. Bring a medium pot of salted water to a boil. Meanwhile, peel the potatoes and cut them into ½-inch pieces. Add them to the boiling water and cook until crisp when pierced with a fork, about 4 minutes. Drain and set aside.

2. To prepare the pork loin, cut it into ¼-inch-thick slices with a sharp knife. Stack several of these slices on top of each other, then slice them into ¼-inch-wide matchsticks. Continue with all the pork, then set the meat aside.

3. Heat a wok or a large skillet (preferably nonstick) over high heat. Swirl in the oil, then add the scallions, garlic, and ginger. Stir-fry for 20 seconds, tossing constantly; then add the pork and stir-fry for 2 minutes. Add the potatoes and cook for 2 minutes, stirring and tossing constantly. Stir in the hot bean paste and sweet bean paste; toss just until melted, then stir in the mirin and black vinegar. Cook for 15 seconds, then serve.

Add one of these to the stir-fry:
With the ginger, add 4 dried red Chinese chiles (or more to taste). ✦ With the potatoes, add ½ pound sea scallops, cut in half; or one 6-ounce can preserved Chinese cabbage; or one 5-ounce can sliced water chestnuts, cut in half (add with the potatoes). ✦ With the bean pastes, add one 6½-ounce can clams, drained and rinsed; or one 5-ounce can sliced water chestnuts, drained and rinsed.

Serve this stir-fry over:
basmati rice ✦ brown rice ✦ steamed collard greens ✦ steamed mustard greens ✦ steamed spinach ✦ white rice ✦ wild rice

{MAKES 6 SERVINGS} Pot Roast

Every region in America has a version of pot roast. This one's unabashedly southern—with potatoes, of course. You slow-roast a relatively inexpensive cut of beef that's been smeared with bottled horseradish to tenderize it. You might think horseradish is too spicy, but it melts into the meat and gravy and becomes sweet and a little tangy, not biting at all. Trim any visible fat off the chuck roast, if you want a leaner dish.

One 3½- to 4-pound chuck roast

2 teaspoons salt, or to taste

1 teaspoon freshly ground black pepper, or to taste

2 tablespoons canola or other vegetable oil

1 large onion, thinly sliced

1 quart (4 cups) beef stock

1 teaspoon Kitchen Bouquet or Gravy Master (optional)

⅓ cup bottled horseradish

2½ pounds medium red-skinned potatoes, such as French Fingerlings or Red la Sodas, scrubbed

1½ tablespoons all-purpose flour

¼ cup water

1. Position the rack in the lower third of the oven and preheat the oven to 350°F. Season the roast with the salt and pepper.

2. Heat a Dutch oven or a large oven-safe pot over medium heat. Swirl in the oil, then add the roast. Brown on both sides, about 4 minutes per side, turning with a spatula or tongs. Transfer the roast to a platter.

3. Add the onion and cook until soft and fragrant, about 4 minutes, stirring often. Place the roast and any accumulated juices back in the pot, then pour in the stock and the Kitchen Bouquet, if using. Smear the horseradish over the roast, then bring the stock to a simmer. Cover the pot and place it in the oven. Bake for 1 hour 30 minutes.

4. Add the potatoes to the pot, resting them in the gravy. Bake for an additional hour, or until the meat is fork-tender.

5. Transfer the meat and potatoes to a serving platter, using tongs or a large slotted spoon. If desired, skim all visible fat off the sauce in the pot. Bring the sauce to a simmer over medium-high heat.

6. In a small bowl, whisk together the flour and water, then whisk this mixture into the sauce. Continue whisking just until thickened, about 2 minutes. Season with salt and pepper, if desired. Spoon some of this sauce over the meat and potatoes, then pass the rest alongside.

Reduce the potatoes to 1½ pounds and add 1 pound of any of the following with the remaining potatoes:
carrots, cut into 3-inch sections ✦ parsnips, peeled and cut into 3-inch sections ✦ rutabagas, peeled and cut into 3-inch chunks ✦ sweet potatoes, peeled and cut into 2-inch-thick rounds ✦ turnips, peeled and cut into 3-inch chunks ✦ yellow beets, peeled and cut into 2-inch chunks

Potato-Crusted Cod

{MAKES 4 SERVINGS}

This elegant dish is perfect for a dinner party or a romantic late-night supper. The very thin potato slices crisp around the fish, giving it a golden, baked crust. The potatoes themselves must be long enough to provide you with slices that can wrap around the fish fillets. Have your fishmonger remove the cod's skin. Check the flesh for bones and remove any with a pair of tweezers.

6 tablespoons (¾ stick) unsalted butter, melted

2 large baking potatoes, at least 6 inches long, preferably Russets, scrubbed

1½ pounds cod fillets, skinned and cut into 4 pieces

2 teaspoons salt, or to taste

1 teaspoon freshly ground black pepper

1 teaspoon vegetable oil

1. Place the melted butter in a large bowl. Peel the potatoes and cut them in half lengthwise. With a vegetable peeler, thinly slice the potatoes, starting with the flat, cut side, making long paper-thin slices. Let the slices fall into the melted butter. You may also use a mandoline, fitted with the thinnest slicing blade, but you'll need to run the potatoes lengthwise over the blade, a tricky task with some mandoline grips. Toss the slices to coat with the butter.

2. Lay an 8-inch piece of plastic wrap on the work surface. To build a bed large enough to hold a piece of cod, lay about one quarter of the potato slices on the plastic wrap in a straight row, overlapping each slice halfway with the next. Sprinkle with ½ teaspoon of the salt and ¼ teaspoon of the pepper, then place a cod fillet on top. Gently fold up the ends of the slices to meet on top of the fillet; seal tightly by rolling the fillet lengthwise—use the plastic wrap to help seal the potatoes and hold them in place. Transfer to a platter and repeat with the remaining potatoes, fillets, salt, and pepper. Refrigerate the four potato-wrapped fillets for at least 30 minutes, but not more than 6 hours.

3. Position the rack in the center of the oven and preheat the oven to 400°F. Gently unwrap the fillets, taking care not to disturb the potato crusts.

4. Heat a large oven-safe sauté pan or skillet (preferably nonstick) over high heat until smoking. Swirl in the oil, then add the fillets, potato seam side down. Immediately lower the heat to medium and cook 3 minutes without turning, until the potatoes brown. Carefully turn the fillets with a spatula, then place the skillet in the oven for 5 minutes, or until the fish is cooked through. Serve immediately.

Sprinkle the fillets with any number of herbs before wrapping them in the potatoes. Divide any of these among the fillets:

12 whole fresh basil leaves ✦ 12 whole fresh sage leaves ✦ 2 tablespoons chopped fresh parsley ✦ 2 tablespoons minced fresh chives ✦ 1 tablespoon chopped fresh rosemary ✦ 1 tablespoon crushed celery seeds ✦ 1 tablespoon crushed fennel seeds ✦ 1 tablespoon ground dried porcini mushrooms (grind in a spice grinder) ✦ 1 tablespoon fresh thyme ✦ 2 teaspoons chopped fresh dill ✦ 2 teaspoons chopped fresh tarragon ✦ 2 teaspoons five-spice powder ✦ 2 teaspoons ground ginger ✦ 1 teaspoon caraway seeds ✦ 1 teaspoon prepared wasabi paste ✦ ½ teaspoon crushed red pepper flakes

Potatoes Sarladaise

This is a salty, crunchy, garlicky miracle, named after the town of Sarlat in Périgord, the birthplace of duck confit. Thin slices of potato are fried crisp in duck fat, then topped with duck confit and baked in the oven. If you would rather not render the fat from the confit, you can buy duck or goose fat in cans from many gourmet stores. Use a quarter cup of it to fry the potatoes if you do so, and discard all fat and skin from the duck confit legs. Duck confit is the meat from preserved duck legs. The heavily salted legs are slowly poached over very low heat in duck fat. They are cooled, then packed in the fat, either in jars, tins, or cryovac-sealed packs. Duck confit is most often available at the butcher counter of gourmet markets.

2 pounds baking potatoes, preferably Russets, scrubbed
3 large duck confit legs, about 6 ounces each, fat preserved on the legs
Olive oil as needed
4 garlic cloves, minced
⅓ cup chopped fresh parsley
1 teaspoon salt

1. Peel the potatoes and slice into ¼-inch rounds, using a sharp paring knife, a mandoline, or a sturdy vegetable peeler. Place the rounds on paper towels to absorb excess moisture and starch.

2. Preheat the oven to 400°F. Scrape the white fat off the duck confit legs and place the fat in a large skillet or sauté pan. Pull the skin off the legs and place it in the skillet as well. Reserve the duck legs and their meat.

3. Heat the duck fat and skin in the skillet over medium-low heat until the fat renders and the resulting oil is very hot and the skin begins to sizzle. Discard the skin and add enough olive oil to make ¼ cup fat in the pan. Place half the potato rounds in the pan and fry until golden, about 15 minutes, stirring occasionally and turning once, but gently, so as not to break them. Transfer the rounds to an 8 × 11-inch baking pan, then fry the remaining rounds using the same technique with the remaining oil in the skillet. Meanwhile, remove the meat from the duck legs; tear it into bite-sized pieces and set aside.

4. Sprinkle the potatoes with the garlic, parsley, and salt. Sprinkle the prepared duck meat over the potatoes. Toss gently, then bake for 10 minutes. Toss again and continue baking until the potatoes are crispy and the garlic is fragrant, about 10 more minutes. Serve immediately.

Herbed Potatoes Sarladaise Before baking, add 2 tablespoons chopped fresh tarragon, 2 tablespoons fresh thyme, and 1 tablespoon chopped fresh rosemary along with the parsley, garlic, and salt.

Onions and Potatoes Sarladaise Reduce the amount of Russets to 1 pound. Thinly slice 1 pound onions into rounds, and fry them in the duck fat along with the remaining potatoes.

Root Vegetables Sarladaise Reduce the amount of Russets to 1½ pounds. Thinly slice ½ pound peeled parsnips and ½ pound peeled turnips. Fry them in the duck fat until softened before adding the remaining potatoes.

Simple Roasted Potatoes Omit the duck confit. Fry the potato rounds in ¼ cup olive oil until crispy, as directed in the recipe. Season and bake them as directed.

Traditional Potatoes Sarladaise In Périgord, this dish is most often made with goose confit, a rarity in the United States. If you can find it, substitute 1 large canned goose confit leg for the duck legs. Use ¼ cup of the liquid fat in the can to fry the potatoes.

{MAKES 4 SERVINGS} Potato Skins

Potato skins remain a favorite retro treat. These stuffed skins are both crispy and gooey, filled with cheese and bacon.

4 large baking potatoes (about 1 pound each), such as Russets, scrubbed
8 tablespoons (1 stick) unsalted butter, melted, then cooled
8 strips bacon, fried and drained
4 scallions, green part only, finely chopped (about 4 tablespoons)
1 cup grated Cheddar (about 4 ounces)

1. Position the rack in the center of the oven and preheat the oven to 400°F. Place the potatoes in the center of the rack and bake until soft, for about 1 hour 15 minutes. Remove to a cooling rack until they can be handled easily. Cut in half, then scoop out the flesh, leaving a ¼-inch-thick shell. Reserve the potato filling for another use, such as Gnocchi (page 95); cover and refrigerate for up to 2 days.

2. Position the rack 4 inches from the broiler, then preheat the broiler. Place the potatoes, skin side up, on a baking sheet, then brush each with 1 teaspoon melted butter. Broil for 1 minute, then turn the skins over. Brush the insides of each with 2 teaspoons melted butter. Broil until brown and crisp, about 3 minutes. Keep the broiler going while you fill the skins.

3. Crumble 2 strips bacon into each skin, then sprinkle about 1 tablespoon scallions in each. Top each with ¼ cup shredded cheese.

4. Broil until the cheese is melted, about 2 minutes. Serve immediately.

Fill the crisped potato skins with any number of fillings instead of the bacon, scallions, and Cheddar, including:

canned tuna, sliced red onions, and shredded Cheddar ✦ chopped deli ham, chunk pineapple, and shredded mozzarella ✦ chopped smoked turkey, chopped pecans, and shredded Havarti ✦ jarred pizza sauce, sliced pepperoni, and shredded mozzarella ✦ pitted black olives, chopped canned artichoke hearts, chopped oregano, and crumbled feta ✦ precooked cocktail shrimp, bottled Caesar dressing, and grated Parmigiano-Reggiano ✦ refried beans and shredded Monterey Jack (served with purchased salsa) ✦ sautéed mushrooms, chopped tarragon, a pinch of crushed red pepper flakes, and shredded Gruyère ✦ sliced corned beef, prepared sauerkraut, and Swiss cheese (served with Russian dressing on the side)

Provençal Stew

This tomato-based stew is reminiscent of a simple one often served in the cafés of Vaucluse, the northernmost outpost of Provence. Very aromatic, it's spiked with pastis, an anise-flavored liqueur popular in Provence. For the best taste, use only oil-cured olives, not canned or water-packed.

2 tablespoons olive oil

1 large onion, chopped

2 garlic cloves, minced

1 medium fennel bulb, trimmed and thinly sliced

2 teaspoons chopped fresh rosemary

2 teaspoons salt, or to taste

1/2 teaspoon freshly ground black pepper

One 28-ounce can diced tomatoes, or whole tomatoes, diced, their liquid reserved

1/2 cup dry vermouth or white wine

1 1/2 pounds red-skinned potatoes, such as Red Bliss or French Fingerlings, scrubbed

1 cup pitted, oil-cured black olives (not water-packed)

1/2 cup chopped fresh parsley

1 tablespoon pastis or Pernod

1. Heat a large pot over medium heat. Swirl in the olive oil, then add the onion and cook until soft and fragrant, about 3 minutes, stirring frequently. Add the garlic and cook for 30 seconds. Stir in the fennel and cook for 2 minutes, stirring frequently; then stir in the rosemary, salt, and pepper and cook for 30 seconds. Pour in the tomatoes and their juice, as well as the vermouth. Bring the mixture to a boil.

2. Meanwhile, cut the potatoes into 1-inch cubes. When the stew is boiling, stir them in along with the olives. Reduce the heat to low, cover, and cook until the potatoes are tender when pierced with a fork, about 30 minutes. Stir in the parsley and pastis; serve immediately.

NOTES *You can add any number of vegetables to the stew, so long as you also add ½ cup chicken or vegetable stock. For the last 5 minutes of cooking, add the additional stock and one of the following: 1½ cups spinach leaves, rinsed; 1½ cups Swiss chard, stemmed; 1 cup fresh peas, or frozen peas, thawed; 1 cup broccoli florets; or 1 cup zucchini, thinly sliced.*

You can also add one of the following in the last 5 minutes of cooking: 1 pound mussels, scrubbed and debearded; ½ pound medium shrimp, peeled and deveined; or ½ pound sea scallops, cut in half. If using mussels, discard any that are open and will not close when tapped before cooking, as well as any that do not open after cooking.

Purple Potato and Black Bean Soup

{MAKES 8 SERVINGS}

Rich and satisfying, this potato and bean soup from Latin American is the perfect antidote to North American winters. It makes a lot and freezes well; keep it in a tightly sealed container or a freezer-safe bag in the freezer for up to two months. Thaw it in the refrigerator, then reheat in a saucepan set over low heat and covered, for about 15 minutes, stirring occasionally.

¾ pound dried black beans, picked over and rinsed

3 tablespoons olive oil

2 medium onions, coarsely chopped

1 large green bell pepper, cored, seeded, and coarsely chopped

4 garlic cloves, minced

¾ pound smoked ham, cut into ½-inch dice

2 teaspoons ground cumin

2 teaspoons salt, or to taste

1½ teaspoons fresh thyme

½ teaspoon freshly ground black pepper

One 14½-ounce can diced tomatoes, or whole tomatoes, diced, their juice reserved

1 cup packed fresh cilantro leaves, washed for sand and finely chopped, plus additional for garnish (optional)

2 bay leaves

3 quarts water

1½ pounds purple potatoes, such as All Blues or Blue Prides, scrubbed

2 tablespoons red wine vinegar

3 dashes Tabasco sauce, or more to taste

Sour cream for garnish (optional)

1. Place the beans in a large bowl; cover with water. Soak overnight, or at least 12 hours, discarding any that float to the surface and cannot be stirred back down. Drain and rinse the beans thoroughly; set aside.

2. Heat a large pot or a Dutch oven over medium heat. Swirl in the oil, then add the onions and pepper. Cook just until fragrant, about 3 minutes, stirring frequently. Add the garlic and cook for 30 seconds. Stir in the drained beans, ham, cumin, salt, thyme, and pepper; cook for 1 minute, stirring constantly. Add the tomatoes, cilantro, bay leaves, and water. Bring to a boil, reduce the heat to low, and simmer, partially covered, for 40 minutes, stirring occasionally.

3. Meanwhile, peel the potatoes and cut them into ½-inch pieces. After the soup has simmered for 40 minutes, stir them into the pot; cook, uncovered, until the beans and potatoes are tender, about 50 minutes, stirring occasionally.

4. Discard the bay leaves. Puree 1 quart of the soup in a blender or a food processor until smooth, scraping down the sides of the canister or bowl if necessary. Stir this puree into the soup, then stir in the vinegar and Tabasco sauce. Raise the heat to medium-high and boil the soup until slightly thickened, about 4 minutes. Serve immediately in bowls, with extra chopped cilantro and dollops of sour cream as a garnish, if desired.

Although this soup is good on its own, it can be doctored by any number of toppings, including:

avocados, diced ✦ cucumbers, thinly sliced ✦ radishes, thinly sliced ✦ salsa, sprinkled on top ✦ scallions, thinly sliced ✦ Tiger Sauce, a traditional Asian-style hot sauce

Purple Potato Tamales

{MAKES 12 TAMALES}

These tamales are steamed traditionally in cornhusks, but they're made with a very untraditional (but Latin American) surprise: mashed purple potatoes. They blend with the blue corn masa dough to create a rich, delicious covering for the pork filling, one that's far lighter than the traditional tamale masa. You can find blue corn masa harina and whole cornhusks at Latin American or Mexican markets—or you can order them from the Source Guide (page 251).

Literally "dough flour," masa harina is the base ingredient for tortillas and tamales, as well as a thickener in Latin American stews and sauces. It's made from dried corn kernels cooked in lime water, then ground to a powder. Blue corn masa harina is made from blue corn kernels that have undergone this process.

For the pork filling
1 pound pork tenderloin, trimmed of any
    silverskin
1 teaspoon chili powder
½ teaspoon salt
1 tablespoon vegetable oil
1 small onion, finely chopped
1 teaspoon ground cumin
1⅓ cups bottled barbecue sauce

For the masa dough
1½ pounds purple potatoes, such as Purple Chiefs,
    Caribes, or Purple Peruvians, scrubbed
1 cup blue corn masa harina
½ teaspoon salt
½ cup water
¼ cup canola or other vegetable oil

For the tamales

14 dried cornhusks, or more in case a few tear, soaked in water for 30 minutes
A vegetable steamer or bamboo steamers

1. To make the filling, position the broiler rack 4 inches from the heat source and preheat the broiler. Rub the pork tenderloin with the chili powder and salt; place it on a lipped baking sheet. Broil for 3 minutes, then turn and broil until the meat reaches 155°F when measured with a meat thermometer stuck into the thick part of the tenderloin, about 3 more minutes. If you need to broil it longer, turn it again. Remove the tenderloin from the heat, tent with aluminum foil, and let stand for 10 minutes. Cut the tenderloin into 3 equal sections and shred them with the grain, using two forks.

2. Heat a large skillet or sauté pan over medium heat. Swirl in the vegetable oil, then add the onion and cook until soft and fragrant, about 2 minutes, stirring frequently. Stir in the cumin and cook for 10 seconds, then add the shredded pork and barbecue sauce. Mix well, bring to a simmer, then cover and set aside while you make the masa. (The filling can be made in advance—store, covered, in the refrigerator for up to three days. Let it come back to room temperature before proceeding with the recipe.)

3. To make the masa, bring a medium pot of salted water to a boil. Add the potatoes and cook until tender when pierced with a fork, about 22 minutes. Drain and cool just until you can handle them. Slip off the skins with your fingers or a paring knife. Press the potatoes through a potato ricer into a medium bowl. Stir in the masa harina and salt with a wooden spoon until smooth, then stir in the water and vegetable oil, mixing until the dough is soft but holds its shape when molded, much like Play-Doh.

4. To make the tamales, drain the cornhusks; cut two husks lengthwise into ¼-inch strips. Divide the masa dough into twelve balls, each about the size of an egg.

5. Lay a whole cornhusk, rough side down, on the work surface. Flatten the husk as well as you can, then place a masa ball in the center. Spread the masa dough into a 4 × 5-inch rectangle with your fingers (the rectangle will need to taper toward the narrower end of the husk—the point is to create a small bed for the filling). Spoon ¼ cup pork filling down the middle of the masa rectangle, leaving ½ inch masa on each end. Roll up the tamale, starting with a long side of the husk and rolling the tamale away from you. Don't press down too tight, but do make a compact roll. Gently press the cylinder of masa dough inside the cornhusk closed. Use two of the ¼-inch strips of cornhusk to tie the ends of the tamale closed. Repeat with the remaining husks, masa dough, filling, and cornhusk strips.

6. Place a vegetable steamer or several stacked bamboo steamers over a pot of simmering water. (Use a pot deep enough so the water doesn't evaporate during the long steaming.) Steam the tamales for 20 minutes. You may have to work in batches, depending on how many tamales will fit in the steamers. You may stack the tamales in the steamer, if they fit and the lid can be secured. Let the steamed tamales stand for 5 minutes, then serve.

Barbecued Chicken Tamales Omit the pork tenderloin. Rub the chili powder and salt into 1 pound chicken tenders, cut into ½-inch pieces, or 1 pound boneless, skinless chicken breasts, cut into ½-inch pieces; sauté in 1 tablespoon vegetable oil in a large skillet over medium heat until cooked through, about 2 minutes. Add to the filling mixture.

Barbecued Mushroom Tamales Omit the pork tenderloin. Sauté 1½ pounds mushrooms, cleaned and thinly sliced, in 1 tablespoon vegetable oil with the chili powder and salt in a large skillet set over medium heat, until the mushrooms give off their liquid and it evaporates. Add to the filling mixture.

Barbecued Swiss Chard Tamales Omit the pork tenderloin. Sauté 1½ pounds Swiss chard, washed, stemmed, and torn into chunks, in 1 tablespoon vegetable oil with the chili powder and salt in a large skillet set over medium heat, until the chard wilts, about 3 minutes. Add to the filling mixture.

Thai Purple Corn Tamales Substitute 1 cup satay sauce for the barbecue sauce.

Quesadillas {MAKES 4 SERVINGS}

Look no further for an easy lunch or quick dinner. These savory little tortilla "sandwiches" are rich and satisfying because they're filled with pepper Jack cheese and shiitake mushrooms. Quesadillas are ready in no time, especially if you make the potatoes in advance and keep them covered in the refrigerator until just before you're ready to make the dish.

1 pound large red-skinned potatoes, such as Desirées or All Reds, scrubbed
Eight 10-inch flour tortillas
1½ cups shredded pepper Jack cheese (about 6 ounces)
4 large jarred pimientos, drained and cut into ¼-inch strips
4 large shiitake mushrooms, stemmed, cleaned, and thinly sliced
1 tablespoon plus 1 teaspoon chopped fresh cilantro

1. Bring a medium pot of salted water to a boil. Add the potatoes and cook until tender when pierced with a fork, about 30 minutes. Drain and cool just until you can handle them. Slip the skins off with your fingers or a sharp paring knife. Slice the potatoes into ¼-inch-thick rounds; set aside.

2. To build a quesadilla, lay a tortilla on your work surface. Sprinkle with 3 tablespoons of the cheese, then one quarter of the potato slices, one quarter of the pimiento slices, and one quarter of the shiitake mushrooms. Add 3 more tablespoons cheese and 1 teaspoon chopped cilantro. Top with another tortilla; press gently to seal. Repeat with the remaining ingredients.

3. Heat a griddle or a large skillet over medium heat. Lay a quesadilla on the griddle or in the pan. Cook for 1 minute, or until the cheese starts to melt and the tortilla starts to brown. Gently flip the quesadilla, using a large metal spatula or two smaller ones. (If you're using a skillet, you can place a small heatproof plate over the quesadilla to help you flip it. Holding the plate with one hand, flip the skillet upside down, remove the plate and quesadilla, place the skillet back over the heat, then gently slide the quesadilla back into the pan.) Cook for 1 minute, or until the tortilla browns. Remove from the griddle or pan, and repeat with the remaining quesadillas. Cut them into quarters and serve immediately.

Avocado and Potato Quesadillas Omit the mushrooms. Slice a large avocado, pitted and peeled, into 12 sections. Place 3 slices each on the quesadillas with the other ingredients.

Cheesy Potato Quesadillas Finely grate 6 ounces Asiago cheese and divide it among the quesadillas with the other ingredients.

Fiery Potato Quesadillas Omit the pimientos. Char 2 Jalisco peppers over a gas flame or in the broiler for 3 minutes, turning with tongs or a long-handled fork. Place in a paper bag to steam for 15 minutes; peel, seed, stem, and chop. Place one quarter of the chopped peppers on each quesadillas with the other ingredients.

Shrimp and Potato Quesadillas Omit the pimientos. Place 3 precooked cocktail shrimp on each tortilla, on top of the potatoes.

Spicy Potato Quesadillas Omit the pimientos. Sprinkle 1 tablespoon purchased salsa on each tortilla along with the other ingredients before adding the top tortilla.

Quiche {MAKES 6 SERVINGS}

A delicious Sunday brunch or easy supper, this dish is guaranteed to please every member of your family. The grated potatoes line the baking dish and the savory egg custard partially melts into it as it bakes, creating a crunchy potato crust.

For the crust

1½ pounds baking potatoes, preferably Russets, scrubbed

1 small onion, minced

1 large egg, at room temperature, lightly beaten

1 teaspoon salt

½ teaspoon freshly ground black pepper

¼ cup canola or other vegetable oil, plus additional for the baking dish

Nonstick spray for the baking dish

For the filling

6 slices bacon, fried crisp, drained, then crumbled

1 cup shredded Gruyère, Emmenthaler, or Swiss (about 4 ounces)

6 large eggs, at room temperature

1½ cups half-and-half

½ teaspoon freshly ground black pepper

1. To make the crust, position the rack in the lower third of the oven and pre-heat the oven to 400°F. Spray a 9-inch pie plate with nonstick spray; set aside.

2. Peel the potatoes, then shred them using the large holes of a box grater or a food processor fitted with the shredding blade. Squeeze the potatoes in batches in your hands over the sink to remove any excess water, then place the shredded potatoes in a large bowl. Blend with the onion, egg, salt, and pepper, using a wooden spoon.

3. Press the potato mixture into the prepared pie plate, distributing it evenly along the bottom and up the sides. Press gently but firmly, creating a dense but not watery crust. Bake for 30 minutes, then brush with the oil and bake until brown, about 10 more minutes. Remove the pie plate to a wire rack and cool for 15 minutes. Reduce the oven temperature to 375°F.

4. To make the filling, line the bottom of the potato crust with the bacon, then sprinkle the cheese evenly over the top. In a medium bowl, whisk the eggs, half-and-half, and pepper until well mixed, about 2 minutes. Pour this mixture over the bacon and cheese.

5. Bake for 30 minutes, or until the quiche is set (that is, when a knife inserted into the center comes out clean). Cool on a wire rack for 5 minutes, then serve.

Indian Potato Quiche Omit the bacon and cheese. Spread ½ cup mango chutney on the bottom of the baked crust. Spread one 10-ounce package frozen peas, thawed, over the mango chutney. Whisk 2 teaspoons curry powder into the egg mixture.

Lobster Potato Quiche Reduce the bacon to 3 slices—crumble these over the crust. Arrange 2 cooked lobster tails, cut into 1-inch slices, over the bottom of the baked crust before adding the cheese.

Sausage Potato Quiche Omit the bacon. Arrange 12 slices (about ½ pound) precooked sausage on the bottom of the baked crust before adding the cheese.

Shrimp Potato Quiche Omit the bacon. Arrange 12 medium shrimp (about 35 per pound), peeled and deveined, on the bottom of the crust before adding the cheese.

Southwestern Potato Quiche Omit the Gruyère or Emmenthaler. Spread 1 cup shredded Monterey Jack on the bottom of the quiche. Mix 1 teaspoon ground cumin, ½ teaspoon ground cinnamon, and ¼ teaspoon ground cayenne pepper into the egg mixture.

Raclette {MAKES 4 SERVINGS}

Once raclette was only eaten by the fire. The cheese was placed on the hearth; melted portions were scraped off and served with boiled potatoes and bread. Not much has changed about the dish—except now there are electric, tabletop raclette makers, modern inventions that make this meal easy and fun for everyone. Raclette is a cow's milk cheese similar to Gruyère but somewhat nuttier; it can be found in the cheese section of most supermarkets. If you don't want to buy or rent an electric raclette maker, see the Notes.

1½ pounds yellow-fleshed fingerling potatoes, such as Rattes or Austrian Crescents, or red-skinned fingerling potatoes, such as Ruby Crescents or Russian Bananas, scrubbed
1½ pounds raclette, cut into ½-inch wedges
1 large round of dark bread, cut into 1-inch cubes
2 cups cornichons or gherkin pickles
2 cups other jarred pickled vegetables, such as okra, onions, or green beans

1. Bring a large pot of salted water to a boil. Add the potatoes and cook just until tender when pierced with a fork, about 20 minutes. Drain and cool, then slice the potatoes in half, or into 2-inch segments if the fingerlings are over 5 inches long.

2. Meanwhile, heat the raclette maker according to the manufacturer's instructions. Place several potato segments on each plate. Add a wedge of cheese to each of the raclette maker's pans; let the cheese melt as the manufacturer's instructions indicate.

3. Remove the pans and scrape the cheese onto the plates, either beside the potatoes or on top. Enjoy with the dark bread and various kinds of pickles.

NOTES *In the French Alps, this dish is often finished with an egg. Crack a large egg into a raclette pan, then let it roast in the raclette oven until done. Scrape it and any browned cheese onto the plate to be enjoyed with the remaining pickles, potatoes, and bread.*

If you don't have a raclette oven, you can melt the cheese in the broiler. Position the broiler rack about 5 inches from the heat, then preheat the broiler. Slice the cheese into slightly larger wedges, about ¾ inch thick, and place them on a small, nonstick baking sheet or in a well-seasoned cast-iron skillet. Broil about 2 minutes. When bubbly, remove the sheet or the pan and scrape the cheese onto the potatoes. Repeat with any remaining cheese until all is melted.

Ravioli {MAKES 4 SERVINGS}

These ravioli are perfect with a rich tomato sauce (such as the one that is made for the Lasagna, page 111), the Cilantro Pesto (page 96), the Sage Gorgonzola Sauce (page 97), or a simple topping of melted butter and chopped parsley.

For the filling

1 pound baking potatoes, such as Russets, scrubbed

3 tablespoons olive oil

1 large onion, finely chopped

¼ cup ricotta cheese (regular, low-fat, or fat-free)

2 tablespoons dry vermouth

½ teaspoon grated nutmeg

½ teaspoon salt

½ teaspoon freshly ground black pepper

For the pasta

2 cups all-purpose flour, plus more as necessary

3 large eggs, plus 1 large egg yolk, well beaten, at room temperature

1 teaspoon salt

1. To make the filling, position the rack in the center of the oven and preheat the oven to 400°F. Place the potatoes on the rack and bake until soft, about 1 hour 15 minutes. Cool on a wire rack.

2. Meanwhile, heat a medium skillet or sauté pan over very low heat. Swirl in the oil, then add the onion. Reduce the heat even further and cook for 5 minutes, stirring frequently. Cover and continue cooking for 20 minutes, stirring occasionally, until the onion is caramelized. Do not let them brown.

3. When the potatoes are cool enough to handle, slip off the skins with your fingers or a sharp paring knife. Press the flesh through a potato ricer into a large bowl. Stir in the cooked onion and any pan juices with a wooden spoon.

Stir in the ricotta, vermouth, nutmeg, salt, and pepper until well mixed and smooth; set aside.

4. To make the pasta, mound the flour on a clean work surface and create a well in the mound's middle. Pour the eggs and salt into the well and begin gently mixing them with a fork, occasionally picking up some flour from the wall of the well and incorporating it into the eggs. Continue mixing, picking up more flour as you beat the eggs. Once the eggs are no longer runny, collapse the flour walls into them and begin mixing with your hands. It's sticky work, and may require more flour, depending on the day's humidity and the eggs' viscosity. Once a dough has been formed, scrape the work surface clean and knead the dough until smooth and only slightly sticky, about 5 minutes, adding more flour in 1-tablespoon increments as necessary to keep the dough from sticking.

5. Break the dough into three or four pieces, each about the size of a small lemon. Knead using the widest setting on the pasta machine, passing the dough through seven or eight times and folding it back onto itself each time. Dust with flour as needed. Once the dough is smooth, begin lowering the settings on the pasta machine, one notch at a time, passing the dough through each time without folding it onto itself. After it has passed through on the pasta machine's final, tightest setting, transfer the long strip of pasta dough to a clean, dry, lightly floured work surface. Position the pasta sheet horizontally in front of you.

6. Place 2 teaspoons of potato filling at one end of the pasta sheet, about ½ inch from the top edge. Continue placing filling on the sheet, each dollop spaced 2 inches apart and ½ inch from the top edge, until you reach the other end of the sheet. Moisten the edge of the dough nearest you and fold the sheet up and over, covering the filling. Press between the small filling mounds to seal the dough and release any trapped air. Seal the two long edges of the pasta sheet together. Cut into separate raviolis, using a ravioli cutter, a pastry cutter, or a sharp knife. Place the filled raviolis on a large cookie sheet dusted with flour. Cover with a clean kitchen towel and repeat with the remaining dough and filling.

7. Fill a large pot with salted water and bring it to a boil over high heat. Drop the raviolis into the water and cook for 2 to 3 minutes, just until the pasta is tender. The water may not come back to a boil. The best test for doneness is simply to bite into one—it should be tender but still have some tooth and texture. Drain and serve immediately with the sauce of your choice.

Herbed Potato Ravioli Add 1 tablespoon minced fresh parsley, 2 teaspoons minced fresh rosemary, and 2 teaspoons fresh thyme to the ravioli filling.

Potato and Mushroom Ravioli Reduce the potatoes to ¾ pound. Finely dice 8 cleaned button or cremini mushrooms. Cook them with the onion.

Sun-Dried Tomato and Potato Ravioli Add ¼ cup chopped marinated sun-dried tomatoes to the filling with the ricotta.

{MAKES 4 SERVINGS} # Red Cooking Pork

Red cooking is a Chinese technique of slowly simmering meat and vegetables in a sweetened soy sauce and wine mixture. It's home cooking through and through and a technique perfectly adaptable to a slow-cooker. The meat becomes very tender and the potatoes slowly melt into the sauce. Dried red chiles are available in Asian markets and in the Asian section of some supermarkets. If you can't find them, substitute half a teaspoon chile oil.

1¼ cups chicken stock
⅓ cup soy sauce
¼ cup dry sherry
2 teaspoons sugar
1½ pounds pork loin, trimmed of any excess fat, cut into 2-inch cubes
2 pounds small white potatoes, such as Creamers or Kennebecs, scrubbed,
   peeled, and halved
6 scallions, cut into 3-inch sections
3 dried red Chinese chiles, or to taste
2 garlic cloves, slivered
2 star anise pods
Two 4-inch cinnamon sticks
4-inch piece fresh ginger, peeled and cut into thin matchsticks
Rice or steamed mustard greens, for serving

1. In a medium bowl, whisk together the stock, soy sauce, sherry, and sugar. Set aside.

2. In a 4-quart or larger slow-cooker, combine the pork, potatoes, scallions, chiles, garlic, star anise, cinnamon sticks, and ginger. Mix well to combine. Pour in the sauce, then mix once again to combine.

3. Cook on low for 8 hours, or until the pork is tender. Discard the chiles, star anise, and cinnamon sticks before serving. Serve over rice or even steamed mustard greens, the traditional accompaniment.

Red Cooking Beef Substitute 1½ pounds beef stew meat for the pork. Add 2 tablespoons grated orange zest to the slow-cooker. Cook on low for 9 hours, or until the beef is tender.

Red Cooking Chicken Substitute 1½ pounds frozen boneless, skinless chicken thighs, cut into 2-inch chunks, for the pork. Cook on low for 6 hours.

Red Cooking Pork with Purple Potatoes Increase the sugar to 2½ teaspoons. Substitute 2 pounds purple potatoes, peeled and quartered, for the white potatoes.

Red Cooking Pork with Sweet Potatoes Reduce the sugar to 1 teaspoon. Substitute 2 pounds sweet potatoes, peeled and cut into 2-inch-thick rounds, for the white potatoes.

Red Cooking Tofu Omit the pork. Cook the potatoes and spices in the sauce on low for 4 hours, then add 1 pound extra firm tofu, cut into 1-inch cubes. Cook for an additional 2 hours on low.

Reuben Rolls

No one knows who made the first Reuben sandwich, that concoction of corned beef, sauerkraut, and Swiss cheese. Ours is a pleasant departure thanks to the mashed potatoes that coat the outside of these fried rolls. They're big, so the egg wash and bread crumb coatings are best applied in two roasting pans.

2 pounds medium baking potatoes, such as Russets, scrubbed
½ cup all-purpose flour
3 large eggs, at room temperature
¾ pound thinly sliced corned beef
¼ pound thinly sliced Swiss cheese
1 cup prepared sauerkraut, thoroughly drained and squeezed of any excess liquid
4 cups vegetable oil, for frying
2 tablespoons water
2 cups plain dried bread crumbs
Bottled Russian dressing, for dipping

1. Bring a large pot of salted water to a boil. Add the potatoes and cook until tender when pierced with a fork, about 22 minutes. Drain and cool just until you can handle them. Slip the skins off with your fingers or a paring knife, then press the potatoes through a potato ricer into a large bowl. Stir in the flour and one of the eggs with a wooden spoon to make a soft dough.

2. To make one roll, lay a 12-inch section of plastic wrap on your work surface. Scoop out one quarter of the potato dough; place it in the center of the sheet. Flour your hands and pat the potato dough into a 6 × 9-inch rectangle, about ¼ inch thick. Top it with one quarter of the corned beef (3 ounces) and one quarter of the cheese (1 ounce), leaving a ½-inch border all around the edges. Place ¼ cup sauerkraut in the middle of the meat and cheese, making a line down the center of the roll.

3. Using the plastic wrap as an easy way to handle the soft sticky dough, lift both the edges of the wrap that are parallel with the long edges of the dough. Bring these plastic wrap sides together, thereby enclosing the filling and creating a cylinder out of the dough. Be careful not to roll any plastic wrap up into the roll. Seal the potato-dough seam by pinching it together through the plastic wrap. Seal the ends as well, smoothing them over to make sure they are tight. Repeat to make three more rolls.

4. Heat the oil in a large high-sided skillet or sauté pan set over medium heat until rippling. If desired, clip a deep-frying thermometer to the inside of the pan and let the oil come to 350°F.

5. Meanwhile, lightly beat the remaining 2 eggs with the water and place the mixture in a roasting pan or a large baking dish. Place the bread crumbs in a second roasting pan or large baking dish.

6. Gently unwrap one cylinder and lay it in the egg wash. Carefully roll it around, then transfer it with your hands or two spatulas to the bread crumbs. Gently roll it to coat on all sides; scoop up the bread crumbs with your hands and gently press them onto the ends. Set the roll aside, then repeat with the remaining rolls.

7. Fry the rolls two at a time in the hot oil until golden brown all over, about 2 minutes each side. Drain them on paper towels, then serve immediately with Russian dressing on the side.

Brie Reuben Rolls Substitute ¼ pound Brie, sliced into thin strips, for the Swiss.

Pastrami Reuben Rolls Substitute ¾ pound sliced pastrami for the corned beef.

Salami Reuben Rolls Substitute ¾ pound sliced salami for the corned beef. Cut the salami into strips to fit in the potato-dough roll.

Shrimp Reuben Rolls Substitute ¾ pound medium shrimp, peeled, deveined, cooked, and roughly chopped, for the corned beef.

Smoked Turkey Reuben Rolls Substitute ¾ pound smoked turkey for the corned beef and ¼ pound Havarti for the Swiss.

Rice, Potatoes, and Shrimp

{MAKES 6 SERVINGS}

Here's our take on a simple rice dish that's recently swept across the tides of Japanese faddishness, thanks to a popular home cooking show in Tokyo. This is a savory one-pot meal: the rice cooks with the shrimp, spices, and potatoes—which melt somewhat, turning soft and buttery. Think of it as Japanese arroz con pollo (without the chicken, of course).

2½ cups water

1 pound yellow-fleshed potatoes, preferably Yukon Golds, scrubbed

½ pound medium shrimp (about 35 per pound), peeled, deveined, and roughly chopped

2-inch piece fresh ginger, peeled and cut into matchsticks

2 scallions, minced

1 tablespoon soy sauce

2 cups sushi rice or other short-grain rice, rinsed until the water runs clear

1. Place the water in a medium saucepan or a rice cooker. Peel the potatoes and cut them into ¼-inch dice, letting the pieces fall into the pan or rice cooker as you cut them.

2. Add the shrimp, ginger, scallions, and soy sauce. Stir in the rice, making sure it is completely submerged in the water. If using a saucepan, set it over medium-high heat and bring it to a boil; cover, reduce the heat to low, and cook undisturbed until the rice is tender, about 15 minutes. Let stand without opening for 10 minutes after cooking. If using a rice cooker, close the lid and set it to cook; let it stand unopened for 10 minutes after it has switched to "warm" or "off" (depending on the machine). Serve immediately.

Stir any one or two of the following into the rice before cooking it:
½ pound asparagus, trimmed and cut into 1-inch sections ✦ ½ pound green beans, trimmed and cut into 2-inch sections ✦ ½ pound shiitake mushrooms, stemmed, cleaned, and thinly sliced ✦ one 5-ounce can sliced bamboo shoots, drained ✦ one 5-ounce can sliced water chestnuts, drained ✦ ½ cup rehydrated wakame, chopped ✦ ¼ cup sliced almonds ✦ 2 tablespoons sesame seeds ✦ 2 table-spoons hoisin sauce ✦ 2 teaspoons dark sesame oil ✦ 2 teaspoons oyster sauce

There's no more classic Swiss dish than this hash-brown pancake. It's a down-to-earth meal before or after a long hike, or after a long day at the office. With parboiled potatoes, roesti comes out crisp every time.

1¾ pounds yellow-fleshed potatoes, such as Charlottes or Yukon Golds, scrubbed
1 teaspoon salt, or to taste
4 tablespoons (½ stick) unsalted butter

1. Bring a large pot of salted water to a boil. Meanwhile, peel the potatoes. Add them to the boiling water and cook until still firm when pierced with a fork, just 8 minutes. Drain and cool completely. (The dish may be made up to this point a day in advance. Cover the potatoes and store them in the refrigerator.)

2. Grate the potatoes into a large bowl, using the large holes of a box grater. (Do not use a food processor, or the potatoes will be mushy.) Toss the grated potatoes with the salt.

3. Melt 2 tablespoons of the butter in a 10-inch skillet (preferably non-stick) set over medium heat. When the butter foam subsides, add the grated potatoes all at once. Press them down and toward the edges of the skillet with the back of a wooden spoon, creating an even top across the pancake. Dot the top with 1 tablespoon of the butter, cover, and cook for 5 minutes. Shake the pan once or twice to make sure the potatoes are not sticking.

4. Uncover, then press the grated potatoes with the back of a wooden spoon, making sure they form a cohesive pancake. Cook for 5 more minutes, or until the bottom is golden brown.

5. Place a plate over the roesti, then invert the skillet, holding onto the plate. If necessary, shake the pan, or use a heat-safe spatula to loosen the roesti. Place the empty skillet back over the heat, add the remaining 1 tablespoon butter, and slip the roesti back into the skillet, raw side down. Press down again with the back of a wooden spoon, shaping the roesti into a compact pancake. Cook for 5 more minutes, or until the pancake is golden and crisp. Slide onto a plate, cut into sections, and serve immediately.

Once the roesti is out of the skillet, top it with one or several of the following:
1 cup Quick Applesauce (page 115) ✦ 1 cup sour cream or crème fraîche ✦ 1 pound mushrooms, cleaned and thinly sliced, sautéed in 2 tablespoons unsalted butter for 5 minutes ✦ 2 fried eggs ✦ 6 strips fried bacon ✦ ½ cup strawberry jam ✦ ½ pound cooked chicken or pork sausage ✦ ½ pound smoked salmon

Salade Niçoise

{MAKES 6 SERVINGS}

To be authentic, boil the potatoes the day before and chill them overnight in the refrigerator so they get a slightly gelatinous texture. Since the tuna need only be seared, not cooked through, buy the freshest sushi-grade tuna you can find—then assemble the salad just before you serve it.

1 pound small red-skinned potatoes, such as Desirées or Red Blisses, scrubbed

1 pound small yellow-fleshed potatoes, preferably fingerlings such as Austrian Crescents, scrubbed

½ pound haricots verts, or green beans, trimmed

3 tablespoons sherry vinegar or white wine vinegar

2 tablespoons Dijon mustard

1 garlic clove, crushed

1 teaspoon salt, or to taste

½ teaspoon freshly ground black pepper

¾ cup plus 2 tablespoons olive oil

2 pounds sushi-grade tuna steak

1 large head romaine lettuce, washed and torn

1 small red onion, sliced into paper-thin rings

4 hard-cooked eggs, peeled and quartered

24 large oil-cured black olives (not water-packed)

1. Bring a large pot of salted water to a boil. Add both kinds of potatoes and cook until tender when pierced by a fork, about 17 minutes. (If the potatoes are of different sizes, they will cook at different rates, so test them occasionally while boiling.)

2. Remove the potatoes with a slotted spoon, then add the haricots verts to the boiling water. Cook just until snap-crisp, about a minute. Drain and cool. (You may make the salad up to this point a day ahead. Cover the potatoes and beans separately in the refrigerator.)

3. In a small bowl, whisk the vinegar and mustard until smooth, then whisk in the garlic, salt, and pepper. Continue whisking as you drizzle in the ¾ cup olive oil in the thinnest possible stream. Whisk until the dressing is emulsified, about a minute; set aside.

4. Heat a large skillet (preferably nonstick) over medium-high heat. Swirl in the remaining 2 tablespoons olive oil, then sear the tuna, cooking it for 2 minutes on each side for rare, 3 minutes on each side for medium. Transfer the tuna from the skillet to a cutting board; let stand for 5 minutes.

5. Meanwhile, arrange the romaine leaves on a platter. Top them with the red onion slices, hard-cooked eggs, olives, green beans, and potatoes. Slice the tuna against the grain into ½-inch-thick slices and lay them across the top of the salad in a decorative pattern. Whisk the dressing again to make sure it's emulsified, then drizzle over the salad. Serve immediately.

Top the salad with any number of "nonstandard" ingredients, including:
blueberries ✦ cantaloupe chunks ✦ corn, either fresh off the cob or frozen corn, thawed ✦ crumbled blue cheese ✦ crumbled goat cheese ✦ diced cornichons or pickles ✦ diced pineapple ✦ diced tomatoes ✦ dollops of mango chutney ✦ grated Asiago or Parmigiano-Reggiano ✦ jicama, peeled and cut into matchsticks ✦ orange supremes, fresh, or canned mandarin sections ✦ precooked cocktail shrimp ✦ sliced cucumbers ✦ sliced mango ✦ sliced peaches ✦ steamed baby zucchini ✦ toasted hazelnuts ✦ toasted pecans ✦ toasted walnuts

Salpiçon

This composed salad of beef and purple potatoes originated in Santiago, Chile, where it's often served as a quick lunch. The dressing is a tangy, spicy mix, a good match against all the different textures. Some purple potatoes turn steely gray when cooked, but the color change won't affect the taste of this hearty salad.

1 garlic clove, minced

1 tablespoon chili powder

¼ cup plus 1 tablespoon fresh lime juice

½ teaspoon ground cumin

½ teaspoon salt

1 pound hanger steak, trimmed of any excess fat

2 pounds purple potatoes, such as Purple Peruvians or All Blues, scrubbed

¾ cup white corn kernels (about 1 large ear), or frozen corn, thawed

1 large avocado, peeled, pitted, and cut into ½-inch pieces

6 radishes, thinly sliced

2 scallions, thinly sliced

⅓ cup chopped fresh cilantro

½ cup extra virgin olive oil

½ teaspoon salt

½ teaspoon freshly ground black pepper

4 dashes Tabasco sauce, or to taste

1. In a small bowl, mix the garlic, chili powder, 1 tablespoon of the lime juice, the cumin, and salt until well combined. Massage this mixture into both sides of the hanger steak. Cover and refrigerate the meat for at least 2 hours, but no more than 6 hours.

2. Meanwhile, bring a medium pot of salted water to a boil. Add the potatoes and cook until tender when pierced with a fork, about 20 minutes. Drain and cool, then cut into quarters, or 2-inch chunks, whichever is smaller.

3. Position the broiler rack 4 inches from the heat and preheat the broiler. Place the hanger steak on a large lipped baking sheet. Broil, turning once, about 3 minutes each side for medium. Transfer the steak to a cutting board and let stand for 5 minutes. Cut it in half, then slice each piece into thin strips against the grain, cutting in long strokes with the knife at a 45-degree angle to the cutting board. Place the sliced steak, potatoes, corn, avocado, radishes, and scallions in a large bowl.

4. To make the dressing, place the cilantro and ¼ cup lime juice in a small bowl. Whisk in the olive oil in a thin stream until the dressing is emulsified, about a minute. Stir in the salt, pepper, and Tabasco sauce to taste. Pour the dressing over the salad, toss, and serve immediately.

Add one or two of any of the following to the salad before it's dressed:
3 jarred pimientos, thinly sliced   ✦   1 cup orange supremes or canned mandarin orange sections   ✦   ½ cup chopped toasted pecans   ✦   ½ cup pitted, thinly sliced green olives   ✦   ½ cup pitted, sliced black oil-cured olives (not water packed)   ✦   ½ cup toasted pepitas   ✦   ½ cup toasted sliced almonds   ✦   one 7-ounce can sliced water chestnuts, drained

Scrapple

This frugal Pennsylvania Dutch dish was originally a cornmeal-thickened, polenta-like mush that had meat leftovers or "scraps" in it. The mixture was refrigerated overnight in a loaf pan to set up, then sliced into slabs and fried in butter. Here, mashed potatoes are added as a thickener, creating a smoother, more delicate dish. Keep it in the refrigerator, covered, for up to five days, slicing off and frying sections of the "loaf" as desired.

1½ pounds pork loin, cut into 2 or 3 large pieces
½ pound baking potatoes, such as Russets, scrubbed
1 teaspoon salt
½ teaspoon freshly ground black pepper
1 cup yellow or white cornmeal, preferably stone-ground
2 tablespoons unsalted butter, or more, for frying

1. Line a 9 × 5-inch loaf pan with plastic wrap so that it generously overlaps the sides. Set aside.

2. Place the pork in a large pot, cover with water, and bring to a boil over high heat. Reduce the heat to medium, cover, and simmer until the pork is tender, about 45 minutes. Remove the pork with tongs or a slotted spoon; set aside to cool. Keep the water boiling. (Alternatively, you can use 1¼ pounds leftover pork roast or pork loin.)

3. Peel the potatoes, then cut them into ½-inch pieces. Add them to the water and cook until soft when pierced with a fork, about 9 minutes. Transfer with a slotted spoon to a large bowl, reserving 2 cups of the cooking water.

4. Mash the potatoes with a potato masher or two forks. Chop the meat into ½-inch cubes and add it to the potatoes, along with the salt and pepper. Mix well with a wooden spoon.

5. Bring the 2 cups cooking liquid to a boil in a large saucepan set over medium-high heat. Whisk in the cornmeal; cook until smooth, about a minute. Reduce the heat to low and cook for 5 minutes, stirring frequently. If it begins to scorch, remove it from the heat, stir in ¼ cup water, then return it to very low heat.

6. Stir the mashed potato mixture into the cornmeal mush, then pack this mixture into the prepared loaf pan. Seal with plastic wrap by wrapping the overhanging sides over the top. Chill in the refrigerator for at least 4 hours, or preferably overnight.

7. Turn the scrapple out onto a work surface and slice into ½-inch slabs. (You may slice as much as you want. Reseal the rest in plastic wrap, return it to the loaf pan, and refrigerate up to five days, tightly sealed.) Melt the butter in a large skillet over medium heat. Add as many scrapple slices as will fit in the pan, and fry them until lightly brown and crisp, about 2 minutes per side. Repeat with more butter, as desired, and slices. Serve immediately.

Stir one or two of the following into the mashed potato mixture before it's added to the cornmeal mush:

3 scallions, thinly sliced ✦ 3 carrots, shredded and blanched for 1 minute in a small pot of salted water, then drained ✦ ½ pound button mushrooms, cleaned and thinly sliced, then sautéed in 2 tablespoons butter ✦ one 10-ounce package frozen corn, thawed ✦ one 10-ounce package frozen mixed vegetables, thawed ✦ one 10-ounce package frozen peas, thawed ✦ 2 cups steamed broccoli florets, chopped ✦ 2 cups steamed cauliflower florets, chopped ✦ ½ cup mango chutney, or other chutney ✦ 1 tablespoon Dijon mustard ✦ 4 dashes Tabasco sauce, or to taste

{MAKES 4 SERVINGS} # Shepherd's Pie

Traditionally, shepherd's pie is a casserole of leftover lamb topped with mashed potatoes. This adaptation is a savory beef stew topped with mashed potatoes and made in potato-skin boats.

For the meat filling
2 tablespoons canola or other vegetable oil

1 medium onion, minced

¾ pound lean ground beef

1 tablespoon all-purpose flour

¼ cup dry vermouth or white wine

2 tablespoons Worcestershire sauce

2 teaspoons rubbed sage

1 teaspoon fresh thyme

½ teaspoon salt

½ teaspoon freshly ground black pepper

For the mashed potatoes
4 large baking potatoes (about 1 pound each), preferably Russets, scrubbed

1 large egg, at room temperature

2 tablespoons unsalted butter, at room temperature

2 tablespoons grated Parmigiano-Reggiano (about ½ ounce)

1 tablespoon chopped fresh parsley

1 teaspoon salt

½ teaspoon sweet paprika

½ teaspoon freshly ground black pepper

¼ cup whole milk or heavy cream

For the topping
¼ cup grated Cheddar (about 2 ounces)

1. To make the filling, heat a medium skillet or sauté pan over medium heat. Swirl in the oil, then add the onion and cook until soft and fragrant, about 3 minutes, stirring frequently. Add the ground beef and sauté until it browns, about 5 minutes, stirring frequently and breaking up any clumps with the back of a wooden spoon.

2. Sprinkle the flour over the beef, stir once, then add the vermouth and Worcestershire sauce. Cook for 2 minutes, stirring constantly, then add the sage, thyme, salt, and pepper. Remove from the heat and set aside to cool while you prepare the mashed potatoes. (The filling can be made up to two days in advance. Cover tightly and store in the refrigerator. Allow the filling to come back to room temperature before proceeding with the dish.)

3. To make the mashed potatoes, position the rack in the center of the oven and preheat the oven to 400°F. Place the potatoes in the center of the rack and bake until soft, about 1 hour 15 minutes. Cool on a wire rack and lower the oven temperature to 350°F.

4. Cut the top quarter off each of the baked potatoes and gently scoop the flesh into a large bowl, leaving ⅛ inch of the potato flesh against the skin, or enough so that the skin doesn't collapse or tear. Set the skins aside.

5. Add the egg, butter, Parmigiano-Reggiano, parsley, salt, paprika, and pepper to the scooped-out flesh. Mash with a potato masher, or beat with a mixer at medium speed, until smooth, about 2 minutes, scraping down the sides of the bowl with a spatula. While still mashing or beating the mixture, add the milk or cream in a thin stream. Mash or beat until the mixture will hold its shape when mounded with a spoon, about 4 minutes by hand or 2 minutes with a mixer. Set aside.

6. Divide the ground beef filling among the four potato-skin shells. Top each with one quarter of the mashed potato mixture. Place the filled potato-skin boats on a lipped baking sheet. Bake for 20 minutes, or until the tops are lightly browned.

7. Divide the Cheddar among the potato-skin boats, sprinkling it on top. Bake for 5 more minutes, or until the cheese is melted and gooey. Let stand on the baking sheet for 5 minutes, then serve.

Blue Cheese Shepherd's Pie Omit the Parmigiano-Reggiano and beat ¼ cup crumbled blue cheese into the mashed potato mixture.

Ground Lamb Shepherd's Pie Substitute ground lamb for the ground beef.

Ground Veal Shepherd's Pie Substitute ground veal for the ground beef.

Italian-Spiced Shepherd's Pie Omit the sage. Sauté 2 garlic cloves, minced, with the ground beef. Then stir 2 tablespoons tomato paste, 2 tablespoons chopped fresh parsley, 1 tablespoon chopped fresh rosemary, and 1 tablespoon chopped fresh oregano into the meat mixture.

Shepherd's Pie with Peas Reduce the ground beef to ½ pound and stir 1 cup fresh peas, or frozen peas, thawed, into the meat mixture with the sage.

Southwestern Shepherd's Pie Reduce the ground beef to ½ pound and stir 1 cup corn kernels (if fresh, about 1 large ear—or frozen corn, thawed) into the meat mixture with the vermouth. Omit the sage and thyme; stir 2 tablespoons chili powder into the meat mixture. Top the potato boats with grated Monterey Jack, instead of Cheddar.

Vegetarian Shepherd's Pie Omit the ground beef and sauté 1½ pounds button or cremini mushrooms, cleaned and thinly sliced, with the onion.

Shrimp Balls {MAKES 16 SHRIMP BALLS}

To make these potato-coated shrimp balls, you'll need a mandoline, an extremely sharp slicing tool, fitted with a shoestring blade or the Cook's Helper, a Japanese tool. Both will make thread-thin potato shavings that can coat the sticky shrimp ball, giving it a prickly crust. If you don't have a mandoline, you can make thin slices of potato with the one-millimeter slicing blade on a food processor. You'll then need to cut those thin slices into shoestring strips with a chef's knife. The idea, of course, is to get potato threads that will coat the balls and give them a crunchy crust when they're deep-fried.

1 pound medium shrimp (about 35 per pound), peeled and deveined
2 scallions, green part only, chopped
2 tablespoons minced fresh ginger
2 garlic cloves, minced
2 tablespoons cornstarch
1 tablespoon soy sauce
1 tablespoon dry sherry or white wine
1½ pounds baking potatoes, preferably Russets, scrubbed
2 quarts canola or other vegetable oil, for frying
½ teaspoon salt

1. Place the shrimp, scallions, ginger, and garlic in a food processor fitted with the chopping blade. Pulse until finely chopped. Add the cornstarch, soy sauce, and sherry; pulse again until a gelatinous paste forms.

2. Peel the potatoes. Fill a large bowl halfway with water. Using a mandoline fitted with a shoestring slicing blade, slice the potatoes into tiny threads. (Or attach the potato to the shaft of the Cook's Helper and crank it through the hole, creating shoestring potatoes that can be cut into more manageable 10-inch threads.) Either way, drop the cut shoestrings into the water as they're made.

3. When you're done, remove the shoestrings from the water in batches and squeeze them completely dry in the palms of your hands. They are delicate, so work in small batches. Place the squeezed threads on a large plate.

4. Form a heaping teaspoon of the shrimp mixture into a ball, then roll it in the potato threads to coat it. You may gently press the potato strings into the shrimp mixture to help them adhere.

5. Pour the oil into a 4-quart saucepan or pot. Attach a deep-frying thermometer to the inside of the pan and place over medium-high heat until the oil reaches 350°F. (Alternatively, fill an electric deep-fryer with oil according to the manufacturer's instructions; set the temperature control to 350°F.)

6. Gently lower a shrimp ball into the oil, using a small strainer or a spatula. Let it crisp for a few seconds in the strainer or on the spatula, then let it sink into the oil. Repeat with three more shrimp balls. Fry until golden and crisp, about 4 minutes. Adjust the heat to maintain the oil's temperature.

7. Using the strainer or spatula, transfer the balls to a plate lined with paper towels; drain. Repeat with the remaining shrimp balls, frying them in batches. Sprinkle salt over them and serve immediately.

DIPPING SAUCES

For easy dipping sauces, whisk any of the following together in a small bowl:

Chinese Vinaigrette

¼ cup dark soy sauce or mushroom-flavored soy sauce
¼ cup seasoned rice vinegar
1 teaspoon sesame oil

Easy Ponzu Sauce

¼ cup soy sauce
2 tablespoons rice vinegar
2 teaspoons mirin (sweetened cooking wine)

Seasoned Soy Sauce

⅓ cup soy sauce
2 tablespoons dry sherry or white wine
2 teaspoons minced fresh ginger
2 teaspoons minced scallion, green part only
1 teaspoon chili oil (optional)

For the truly Chinese flavor of a "dry" salt dip, do not salt the shrimp balls when they are finished frying, but mix together the following to use as a dip:

1½ tablespoons salt
1 tablespoon crushed toasted Szechwan peppercorns

Skordalia on Grilled Shrimp

{MAKES 4 SERVINGS}

Skordalia is something of a Greek passion, set out at bars and on dinner tables throughout the country. It's a garlicky puree of potatoes, olive oil, and lemon juice, sometimes served as an appetizer, sometimes used as a sauce. We've chosen the latter and paired this potato sauce with grilled shrimp.

For the shrimp

2 pounds large shrimp (12 to 15 per pound), peeled and deveined

2 tablespoons olive oil

4 garlic cloves, minced

2 teaspoons chopped fresh oregano

1 teaspoon salt, or to taste

½ teaspoon freshly ground black pepper

For the skordalia

1 large garlic head, unpeeled

1 pound baking potatoes, such as Russets, scrubbed

½ cup extra virgin olive oil

½ cup yogurt (regular, low-fat, or fat-free)

2 tablespoons lemon juice

1 teaspoon salt

½ teaspoon freshly ground black pepper

1. Marinate the shrimp by placing them in a large glass, ceramic, or stainless steel bowl and tossing them with the olive oil, garlic, oregano, salt, and pepper. Cover and refrigerate for at least 30 minutes, but no more than 24 hours.

2. To make the skordalia, position the rack in the center of the oven and preheat the oven to 400°F. Slice the top quarter off the garlic head, exposing all the cloves. Discard this smaller part and wrap the remaining head in aluminum foil, sealing it tightly. Bake for 45 minutes, or until the garlic is soft and fragrant. Unwrap to cool and set aside.

3. Bring a large pot of salted water to a boil. Meanwhile, peel the potatoes and cut them in half. Add them to the boiling water, then cook until soft when pierced with a fork, about 25 minutes. Transfer them with a wooden spoon to a plate, set aside to cool for 10 minutes, then press them through a potato ricer into a medium bowl. Mix in the olive oil, yogurt, lemon juice, salt, and pepper with a wooden spoon. Squeeze the softened garlic cloves from their husks into the bowl; mix until smooth and creamy. Set aside at room temperature while you prepare the shrimp. (Do not refrigerate—the potatoes will become gummy and the oil will solidify.)

4. Light the charcoal of a barbecue grill or preheat a gas grill. (Alternatively, position the broiler rack 4 inches from the heat and preheat the broiler.)

5. Place the shrimp on the grilling rack and grill about 2 minutes per side, just until firm and pink. (If using a broiler, lay them on a baking sheet and broil until pink and firm, about 2 minutes per side.) Serve 6 to 7 shrimp per person, on a bed of ½ cup skordalia sauce.

There are as many versions of this sauce as there are Greek islands. Stir any of the following into the skordalia:
½ cup ground almonds ✦ ½ cup ground walnuts ✦ ¼ cup chopped parsley ✦ 1 tablespoon white wine vinegar ✦ ¼ teaspoon ground cayenne pepper ✦ 4 anchovy fillets, minced

Skordalia also works well over grilled lamb chops. Buy 8 rib or shoulder chops and marinate them in a double batch of the olive oil marinade used for the shrimp. Grill the chops about 90 seconds per side for rare, 2 minutes for medium. (Alternatively, broil them about 2 minutes per side for rare, 3 minutes for medium.)

Smoked Pork Chops with Sauerkraut and Potatoes

{MAKES 4 SERVINGS}

This simple, one-pan meal is not a wintry dish at all. It's surprisingly light, thanks to the sauerkraut, which brightens the taste considerably. Smoked pork chops and prepared sauerkraut are available at the butcher counter of most markets. Serve with crusty bread and a glass of cold German beer.

2 pounds prepared sauerkraut
1 teaspoon caraway seeds
7 juniper berries, crushed with the side of a chef's knife or the bottom of a pot
4 thick-cut smoked pork chops, about ¾ pound each
2 pounds small red-skinned potatoes, such as All Reds or Huckleberries, scrubbed
½ cup apple juice or apple cider

1. Position the rack in the center of the oven and preheat the oven to 350°F.

2. Mix the sauerkraut, caraway seeds, and juniper berries in a 10-inch covered casserole dish or a large, high-sided, oven-safe sauté pan. Nestle the pork chops into this mixture, then add the potatoes, pressing them lightly into the sauerkraut. Pour the apple juice over the top.

3. Cover and bake for 1 hour 15 minutes, or until the potatoes are tender when pierced with a fork, the sauerkraut is bubbling, and the meat is nearly falling off the bones. Serve immediately.

Brats and Smoked Pork Chops Add 2 boiled bratwursts, cut into thirds, to the casserole. You'll need to use a 12-quart casserole dish.

Hearty Smoked Pork Chops Omit the apple juice and pour ⅔ cup dark beer over the dish before baking.

Smoked Pork Chops with Apples Reduce the sauerkraut to 1 pound. Stir 1 pound apples, shredded, into the remaining sauerkraut mixture.

Spicy Smoked Pork Chops Stir 2 tablespoons bottled horseradish into the sauerkraut mixture before topping with the pork chops.

Tomatoes and Smoked Pork Chops Stir 1 cup diced tomatoes into the sauerkraut mixture before adding the pork chops.

Smoked Salmon Potato Salad

{MAKES 6 SERVINGS}

Barbara Lauterbach's book Potato Salad establishes her as queen of the dish. This easy salad, inspired by one of her inventive concoctions, is made with smoked salmon, then tossed with a mayonnaise/sour cream dressing. It's even better the day after it's made. Buy the freshest smoked salmon you can find, preferably hand cut to order.

2 pounds small red-skinned potatoes, such as Red Blisses or Ruby Crescents, scrubbed

8 ounces smoked salmon, cut into ¼-inch strips

1 small red onion, minced

1 celery stalk, minced

2 tablespoons capers, drained and rinsed

2 tablespoons finely chopped dill

⅓ cup mayonnaise (regular, low-fat, or fat-free)

⅓ cup sour cream (regular, low-fat, or fat-free)

1 tablespoon bottled horseradish, or to taste

3 tablespoons white wine vinegar

1 teaspoon salt, or to taste

½ teaspoon freshly ground black pepper

1. Bring a medium pot of salted water to a boil. Add the potatoes and cook until tender when pierced with a fork, about 20 minutes. Drain and cool slightly, then cut them into quarters. Place them in a large bowl; add the salmon, onion, celery, capers, and dill. Gently toss, taking care not to mash the potatoes.

2. In a small bowl, whisk the mayonnaise, sour cream, and horseradish until smooth. Whisk in the vinegar, salt, and pepper. Whisk in more horseradish if you prefer a spicier dressing—but taste before you add more, for horseradish can easily overpower the salad.

3. Pour the dressing over the potato salad, then toss it gently, just until combined. This salad may be made ahead of time; store it tightly covered in the refrigerator for up to 2 days. Allow the salad to come back to room temperature before serving.

Add one or two of any of the following to the salad before it's dressed:
1 cup cooked broccoli florets ✦ 1 cup cooked peas ✦ 1 cup cooked corn kernels ✦ ½ cup chopped dates ✦ ½ cup chopped fresh cherries ✦ ½ cup orange supremes, or blood orange supremes, or canned mandarin orange sections ✦ ½ cup diced pear ✦ ¼ cup dried cranberries ✦ ¼ cup raisins or currants ✦ 1 tablespoon corn relish ✦ 1 tablespoon pickle relish ✦ 2 teaspoons chopped parsley ✦ 1 teaspoon thyme ✦ 4 dashes Tabasco sauce, or to taste

Soufflé

Despite the reputation soufflés have for being difficult, this sophisticated meal is a snap to make. Potatoes add depth to this lighter-than-air, egg-white concoction. Bring the eggs to room temperature and make sure the whites have not one speck of yolk in them.

Unsalted butter, at room temperature, for greasing the soufflé dish
1 pound white potatoes, such as Kennebecs or Irish Cobblers, scrubbed
½ cup heavy cream
3 large eggs, separated, plus 2 large egg whites, at room temperature
½ cup grated Parmigiano-Reggiano (about 2 ounces)
1 teaspoon salt, or to taste
½ teaspoon freshly ground black pepper
¼ teaspoon grated nutmeg

1. Position the rack in the center of the oven and preheat the oven to 450°F. Generously butter the sides and bottom of a 6-cup soufflé dish; set aside.

2. Bring a medium pot of salted water to a boil. Meanwhile, peel the potatoes and cut them in half. Add them to the boiling water and cook until soft when pierced with a fork, about 25 minutes. Drain and cool slightly, then press them through a potato ricer into a large bowl. Beat in the cream with an electric mixer set at medium speed, then beat in 3 egg yolks, the grated Parmigiano-Reggiano, salt, pepper, and nutmeg just until light and fluffy, about 2 minutes. Set aside.

3. Place the 5 egg whites in a large clean bowl. Clean the beaters and dry them thoroughly, then beat the whites with the mixer at high speed until stiff peaks form, about 5 minutes.

4. Fold one third of the beaten egg whites into the potato mixture with a rubber spatula. Then very gently fold in the remaining beaten egg whites. You don't want to lose the whites' volume, so use with a gentle, circular motion, starting at the bottom of the mixture and carefully turning it onto the top. Do not overmix—there may be small pockets of unincorporated egg whites throughout.

5. Pour into the buttered soufflé dish, place in the oven, and immediately reduce the oven temperature to 375°F. Bake for 30 minutes, or until the soufflé is puffed and brown. Serve immediately.

Cheddar and Bacon Potato Soufflé Omit the Parmigiano-Reggiano. Use ½ cup grated Cheddar (about 2 ounces) instead. Fold 4 bacon strips, fried and finely crumbled, into the potato mixture before adding the egg whites.

Chestnut and Potato Soufflé Reduce the potatoes to ¾ pound. Mash ¾ cup jarred steamed chestnuts with the cooked potatoes.

Garlicky Potato Soufflé Mash 1 head roasted garlic (see page 195) into the potato mixture, along with 3 tablespoons minced chives, before folding in the egg whites.

Mexican Potato Soufflé Omit the Parmigiano-Reggiano and the nutmeg. Add ½ cup finely grated Monterey Jack (about 2 ounces), 2 teaspoons ground cumin, ½ teaspoon ground cinnamon, and 4 (or more) dashes Tabasco sauce to the potato mixture.

Southern Potatoes and Greens Casserole

{MAKES 4 SERVINGS}

This casserole is made up of layers of potatoes and greens, covered in a thick cheesy sauce, and baked until bubbling. It's a classic dish from the low-lying areas north of the Gulf Coast.

1½ pounds yellow-fleshed potatoes, such as Yukon Golds or Ozettes, scrubbed

1 pound collard greens, or mustard greens, or the two mixed, washed, stemmed, and shredded

4 tablespoons unsalted butter, plus additional for greasing the casserole dish, at room temperature

8 strips bacon

1 large onion, chopped

2 teaspoons minced oregano

1 teaspoon celery seed

2 tablespoons all-purpose flour

1½ cups milk (regular or low-fat, but not fat-free)

1½ cups shredded Swiss cheese (about 6 ounces)

½ teaspoon salt

½ teaspoon freshly ground black pepper

4 dashes Tabasco sauce, or to taste

1. Bring a medium pot of salted water to a boil. Meanwhile, cut the potatoes into ¼-inch-thick slices. Add them to the boiling water, then cook until tender when pierced with a fork, about 7 minutes. Transfer them with a slotted spoon to a colander, then add the greens to the pot and cook until tender, about 3 minutes. Drain, cool, and blot dry with paper towels.

2. Melt 1 tablespoon of the butter in a large skillet set over medium-high heat. Add the bacon and fry until crisp, about 4 minutes, turning once. Transfer the bacon to a plate lined with paper towels to drain. Reserve the bacon drippings in the skillet.

3. Position the rack in the center of the oven and preheat the oven to 350°F. Butter a 10-cup casserole dish, au gratin dish, or baking pan. Place one quarter of the potato slices in the dish, then lay one quarter of the greens on top of them. Crumble 2 strips bacon over the greens. Make three more potato-greens-bacon layers, then set the casserole aside.

4. Place the skillet with the bacon drippings over very low heat, then melt the remaining 3 tablespoons butter in it. Add the onion and cook until golden and sweet, about 15 minutes, stirring often. Reduce the heat if the onion starts to brown. Stir in the oregano and celery seed, then the flour. Cook for 10 seconds, then whisk in the milk in a thin steady stream. Continue whisking until the mixture bubbles and thickens, about a minute. Take the skillet off the heat and stir in the cheese, salt, pepper, and Tabasco sauce. Pour this mixture over the potatoes and greens in the casserole.

5. Bake for 40 minutes, or until bubbling and lightly browned. Cool on a wire rack for 5 minutes, then serve.

Potatoes and Chard Casserole Substitute 1 pound red or white chard, washed, stemmed, and shredded, for the collard greens.

Potatoes and Kale Casserole Substitute 1 pound kale, washed, stemmed, and shredded, for the collard greens. Cook it in the boiling water about 5 minutes.

Potatoes, Crawfish, and Greens Casserole Divide ½ pound crawfish meat among the layers of potatoes and greens.

Potatoes, Sausage, and Greens Casserole Divide ½ pound cooked, sliced sausage among the layers in the casserole.

Potatoes, Shrimp, and Greens Casserole Place ¼ pound medium shrimp (about 35 per pound), peeled, deveined, and roughly chopped, on top of each layer of greens (you'll need 1 pound of shrimp in all).

{MAKES 4 SERVINGS} # Spanish Omelet

An omelet with fried potatoes is typical fare in Madrid's many bars—not fried potatoes on the side, but packed inside, a great contrast to the fluffy eggs. A cast-iron pan, well seasoned from much use, or a nonstick skillet without a nick on it makes it easy. If you can't find chorizo, don't despair—just make the dish with or without any smoked sausage.

1 pound white potatoes, such as Katahdins or Maris Pipers, scrubbed

3 tablespoons olive oil

1 small onion, minced

1 small green bell pepper, cored, seeded, and finely chopped

One 15-ounce can diced tomatoes, or whole tomatoes, diced, their juice
  reserved

One 6-ounce jar pimientos, drained and rinsed

1/3 cup sliced pitted green olives

1 tablespoon chopped fresh oregano

1/2 teaspoon crushed red pepper flakes

1/2 teaspoon salt

1/4 pound dried Spanish chorizo, halved, then cut into 1/4-inch dice

8 large eggs, well beaten, at room temperature

1. Bring a medium pot of salted water to a boil. Meanwhile, peel the potatoes and cut them into 1/2-inch dice. Add them to the boiling water and cook until they are tender when pierced with a fork, about 7 minutes. Drain and set aside.

2. Before you make the omelet, make the sauce that will be poured over it. Heat a small saucepan over medium heat. Swirl in 2 tablespoons of the olive oil, then add the onion and green pepper. Cook until fragrant, about 4 minutes; then add the tomatoes, pimientos, olives, oregano, red pepper flakes, and salt. Reduce the heat to low and cook until the mixture thickens slightly, about 5 minutes, stirring occasionally. Set aside but keep warm on the back of the stove.

3. Heat a large well-seasoned cast-iron skillet or a large nonstick skillet over medium-high heat. Swirl in the remaining 1 tablespoon olive oil, then add the chorizo. Cook for 2 minutes, just until it begins to render its grease, then add the cooked potatoes. Cook for 5 minutes, stirring only once or twice. You want the potatoes to crisp, but not stick to the pan.

4. When the potatoes are crispy, reduce the heat to medium and pour in the eggs. Cook undisturbed for 30 seconds, then begin pulling back the sides of the omelet with a wooden spoon or a heat-safe rubber spatula. As you gently pull back the sides to the middle, tip the pan so that some raw egg mixture flows into the open space. As you're doing this, shake the pan to make sure the omelet is loose, not stuck. If it is, let it get a little more set, then gently run the heat-safe spatula or a knife under it, making sure not to tear the omelet. Continue pulling back the edges of the omelet and letting some of the raw egg flow into the open space. Once the bottom is firm, shake the pan vigorously to loosen the omelet—you may need to pick it up and rap its sides with your hand (protected, of course, by an oven mitt or hot pad). Cook for another 20 seconds, just until the top is set. (It can still be a little runny because it will cook as you fold it over.)

5. To get the omelet out of the pan, tip the pan up and let the omelet fall down just a little to one side of the pan. Place a serving plate underneath the pan, then jiggle half of the omelet over the rim of the skillet and onto the plate, taking care not to break the omelet. Once part of it is resting on the plate, flip the skillet up and over, so that the omelet folds onto itself as it comes out of the pan. Top with the reserved sauce; serve immediately.

Cheesy Spanish Omelet Sprinkle 1 cup grated Manchego or Asiago (about 4 ounces) over the top of the omelet once it begins to set in the pan.

Purple Potato Spanish Omelet Substitute purple potatoes for the Russets.

Saffron Spanish Omelet Add ⅛ teaspoon crumbled saffron threads to the pan with the chorizo.

Spanish Omelet with Clams Stir one 6½-ounce can clams, drained and rinsed, into the sauce with the tomatoes.

Spanish Omelet with Peas Add 1 cup fresh peas, or 1 cup frozen, thawed, to the skillet just before you pour in the eggs.

Spanish Omelet with Shrimp Lay 8 precooked cocktail shrimp down the middle of the top of the omelet before pouring on the reserved sauce.

Spanish Potato Salad {MAKES 4 SERVINGS}

This simple potato salad is made with chorizo, chickpeas, pimientos, and fresh vegetables, dressed in a saffron vinaigrette. It's light and satisfying, easy to make and pretty to serve. If you can find only Mexican-style chorizo (see page 11), slice it into ½-inch sections and fry it in the oil until it is cooked, about 5 minutes.

For the salad

1¾ pounds small yellow-fleshed potatoes, such as German Butterballs, Charlottes, or small Yukon Golds, scrubbed

1 tablespoon olive oil

1 pound dried Spanish chorizo, cut in half lengthwise, then into ½-inch sections

One 14-ounce can chickpeas, drained and rinsed

3 jarred pimientos, drained and cut into thin strips

1 small red onion, thinly sliced

3 celery stalks, chopped

¼ cup chopped fresh parsley

For the dressing

⅛ teaspoon saffron threads

1 tablespoon hot water

3 tablespoons sherry vinegar or white wine vinegar

1½ teaspoons anchovy paste

½ teaspoon freshly ground black pepper

½ cup extra virgin olive oil

Salt to taste

1. To make the salad, bring a medium pot of salted water to boil. Add the potatoes and boil until tender when pierced with a fork, about 14 minutes. Drain and cool slightly, then cut in half, or in 1-inch chunks, whichever is smaller. Place in a large serving bowl.

2. Heat a medium skillet or sauté pan over medium heat. Swirl in the oil, then add the chorizo. Cook until golden brown, about 2 minutes, stirring frequently. Transfer with a slotted spoon to a plate lined with paper towels to drain.

3. Add the chorizo to the potatoes, along with the chickpeas, sliced pimientos, onion, celery, and parsley. Stir with a wooden spoon to combine.

4. To make the dressing, crumble the saffron threads in a small bowl, pour in the hot water, and soak for 5 minutes. Whisk in the vinegar, anchovy paste, and pepper until smooth. Continue whisking as you drizzle in the olive oil in a slow, steady stream. Whisk until emulsified, about a minute. Season with salt, if desired. Pour over the potato salad, gently toss, and serve immediately.

Add one or two of any of the following to the potato mixture before it's dressed:
12 cherry tomatoes, halved ✦ 6 steamed asparagus spears, cut into 1-inch pieces ✦ 1 cup cooked peas, drained and cooled ✦ ½ cup chopped precooked cocktail shrimp ✦ ½ cup orange supremes or canned mandarin orange sections ✦ ½ cup raisins or currants ✦ ½ cup sliced grapes ✦ ½ cup sliced green onion ✦ ½ cup sliced radishes ✦ ½ cup sunflower seeds ✦ ½ cup toasted pine nuts ✦ ½ cup toasted sliced almonds ✦ ¼ cup chopped fresh cilantro ✦ 2 tablespoons capers, drained and rinsed

Split Pea Soup {MAKES 8 SERVINGS}

The starch from the potatoes naturally thickens this stock, while the potatoes remain toothsome, a nice texture contrast to the peas. For a heartier dish, try any of the variations below—but the original recipe is strictly vegetarian. This soup can be made ahead and kept, tightly covered, in the refrigerator for up to three days. Bring it back to room temperature and use a little more stock to thin it out before reheating.

3 tablespoons unsalted butter
1 large onion, finely chopped
4 medium carrots (about ¾ pound), cut into ½-inch rounds
2 celery stalks, finely chopped
1 teaspoon fresh thyme
½ teaspoon rubbed sage
1 pound green or yellow split peas, rinsed
8 cups (2 quarts) vegetable stock, plus more to thin the stew if necessary
1 bay leaf
2 pounds yellow-fleshed potatoes, preferably Yukon Golds, scrubbed
½ teaspoon salt, or to taste
½ teaspoon freshly ground black pepper
2 teaspoons lemon juice (optional)

1. Melt the butter in a large pot set over medium heat. Add the onion, carrots, and celery; cook until soft and fragrant, about 4 minutes, stirring often. Stir in the thyme and sage, cook for 15 seconds, then stir in the split peas, stock, and bay leaf. Bring the mixture to a boil, reduce the heat to low, and simmer, covered, for 30 minutes, stirring occasionally.

2. Meanwhile, peel the potatoes and cut them into ½-inch pieces. Add them to the pot. Cover and simmer for 1 hour, stirring often so that the soup doesn't scorch. If the mixture becomes too thick, add ½ cup stock, or more, to thin it out. Once the potatoes are tender, season the dish with salt, pepper, and lemon juice, if desired. Discard the bay leaf and serve immediately.

Mushroom Split Pea Soup Sauté 2 pounds cremini or button mushrooms, cleaned and sliced, in 2 tablespoons butter until they release their liquid; stir them and any pan drippings into the soup with the salt and pepper.

Split Pea and Mixed Vegetable Soup Stir an extra ¼ cup stock and one 10-ounce package frozen mixed vegetables, thawed, into the soup after the potatoes are tender. Cook for an additional 5 minutes.

Split Pea Soup with Bacon Reduce the butter to 1 tablespoon. Cut the bacon into 1-inch strips, then fry them in the butter before adding the onion, carrots, and celery.

Split Pea Soup with Canadian Bacon Stir ½ pound thickly sliced Canadian bacon, cut into 1-inch pieces, into the soup with the potatoes.

Split Pea Soup with Chorizo Reduce the butter to 2 tablespoons. Slice ½ pound dried Spanish chorizo in half lengthwise, then into ½-inch half-moons. Fry them in the butter before adding the onion, carrots, and celery.

Split Pea Soup with Ham Add 1 pound ham hocks or a large ham bone (with meat still attached) with the potatoes.

Split Pea Soup with Pancetta Reduce the butter to 1 tablespoon. Cut ⅔ pound pancetta into ½-inch cubes. Fry it in the butter before adding the onion, carrots, and celery.

Split Pea Soup with Turkey Sausage Reduce the butter to 2 tablespoons. Cut ¾ pound turkey sausage into ½-inch-thick slices. Fry them in the butter until brown, then add the onion, carrots, and celery.

Steak Frites {MAKES 4 SERVINGS}

There's no more classic French bistro dish than steak frites. To make four great steaks at home, you'll need two cast-iron skillets, or an outdoor barbecue grill. If you like, make these shoestring fried potatoes on their own, a perfect side to other roast meats or fish. You'll need either a professional mandoline fitted with the shoestring blade or a Cook's Helper, a Japanese cutting tool (see Source Guide, page 251).

For the shoestring fries

3 quarts peanut or canola oil

2 pounds yellow-fleshed potatoes, such as Bintjes, Rattes, or Yukon Golds, scrubbed

2 teaspoons salt, or to taste

For the steaks

Four 12-ounce strip steaks, trimmed of any excess fat

2 teaspoons salt, preferably coarse-grained or kosher

1 teaspoon freshly ground black pepper

2 tablespoons plus 2 teaspoons canola or other vegetable oil

1. To make the fries, pour the oil into a 6-quart pot. Clip a deep-frying thermometer to the inside of the pot and heat the oil over medium-high heat to 325°F. (Alternatively, fill an electric deep-fryer with oil and set the temperature control to 325°F.)

2. Meanwhile, peel the potatoes and slice them into shoestrings, using either a mandoline fitted with the shoestring blade or a "Cook's Helper" that pins them to a rod and cranks them through a shoestring hole. If you use this latter method, slice the long potato threads into manageable shoestrings 8 to 10 inches long.

3. Fry the potatoes in handful batches until crisp, about 3 minutes. Stir them once or twice to prevent them from sticking to the sides of the pot or each other. Transfer from the oil with a slotted spoon or a long-handled strainer to a plate lined with paper towels; season with salt while they're still warm.

4. To make the steaks, position the oven rack in the lower third of the oven and preheat the oven to 475°F. Rub each steak with ½ teaspoon salt, ¼ teaspoon pepper, and 2 teaspoons olive oil.

5. Place two cast-iron skillets over high heat. Allow them to heat until they are smoking, about 5 minutes. Place two steaks in each pan; cook for 1 minute, then turn with a spatula or tongs. Place the skillets with the steaks in the oven. Roast until they reach the doneness you desire, about 3 minutes for rare, 5 minutes for medium. Transfer the steaks to a cutting board or to four dinner plates and let stand for 5 minutes, then serve with the frites.

Season the steaks in any number of ways. Omit the pepper, then divide the following among the steaks:

2 tablespoons plus 2 teaspoons chili powder (2 teaspoons each) ✦ 2 tablespoons plus 2 teaspoons chopped fresh rosemary (2 teaspoons each) ✦ 2 tablespoons plus 2 teaspoons ground dried porcini mushrooms (2 teaspoons each) ✦ 2 teaspoons crushed toasted Szechwan peppercorns (½ teaspoon each) ✦ 2 teaspoons curry powder (½ teaspoon each) ✦ 2 teaspoons hot Hungarian paprika (½ teaspoon each) ✦ 2 teaspoons crushed pink peppercorns (½ teaspoon each) ✦ 2 teaspoons cracked black peppercorns (½ teaspoon each)

Steamed Mussels and Potatoes

{MAKES 4 SERVINGS}

This Portuguese-inspired stew combines briny mussels, salty pancetta, and waxy potatoes in a thyme-scented broth. Use the mussels the day you buy them; store them under a damp paper towel in your refrigerator. If you can't find diced canned tomatoes at your market, cut up whole canned tomatoes with a pair of kitchen shears while they're still in the can.

2 tablespoons olive oil

½ pound pancetta, cut into ½-inch chunks

1 large onion, roughly chopped

2 celery stalks, cut into 1-inch pieces

1 pound yellow-fleshed fingerlings, such as Austrian Crescents or Russian
  Bananas, or Yukon Golds, scrubbed

2 garlic cloves, minced

2 tablespoons fresh thyme

½ teaspoon crushed red pepper flakes

½ teaspoon salt

One 28-ounce can diced tomatoes, their juice reserved

½ cup dry vermouth

2 pounds mussels, scrubbed

1. Heat a large pot over medium heat. Swirl in the oil, then add the pancetta and cook until browned, about 3 minutes, stirring often. Add the onion and celery; cook until softened, about 3 minutes, stirring frequently.

2. Meanwhile, cut the potatoes into ½-inch chunks. Stir them into the pan, along with the garlic, thyme, red pepper flakes, and salt. Cook for 1 minute, just until heated through. Pour in the tomatoes, along with their juice, and the vermouth. Cover, reduce the heat to low, and simmer until the potatoes are tender when pierced with a fork, about 7 minutes. Stir the dish occasionally to prevent scorching.

3. Meanwhile, debeard the mussels by pulling off the small wiry threads that protrude from the shell. Discard any mussels that do not close when tapped.

4. When the potatoes are tender, stir the stew well, then add the mussels. Cover and simmer until they open, about 5 minutes. Discard any mussels that do not open and serve immediately in large bowls.

Fiery Mussels and Potatoes Stir in 2 fresh serrano chiles, chopped, with or without the seeds, or 1 fresh jalapeño pepper, chopped, with or without its seeds, with the potatoes.

Green-and-Red Mussels and Potatoes Substitute a 14-ounce can diced tomatoes for the 28-ounce can. Add two 5-ounce cans tomatillos, drained and diced, and ½ cup water with the tomatoes.

Mussels, Escarole, and Potatoes Omit the celery. Add 1 bunch escarole, cleaned and roughly chopped (about 3 cups), with the tomatoes.

Mussels, Fennel, and Potatoes Omit the celery. Add 1 small fennel bulb, diced, with the onions.

Sausage, Mussels, and Potatoes Substitute ½ pound diced sausage for the pancetta. You might use chorizo, sweet Italian, or chicken and sage sausage.

Stuffed Peppers {MAKES 6 SERVINGS}

These aren't your traditional stuffed peppers. They are instead stuffed with a spicy sweet potato puree, then topped with cheese. Pepitas are pumpkin seeds, sold in Latin American and Mexican markets.

3 pounds sweet potatoes, such as Jewels or Red Garnets, scrubbed

6 large green or red bell peppers

6 tablespoons pepitas

3 tablespoons unsalted butter, at room temperature

1 large onion, chopped

1 celery stalk, chopped

6 tablespoons packed light brown sugar

3 tablespoons chili powder

1½ teaspoons salt, or to taste

1 teaspoon freshly ground black pepper

1½ cups shredded Cheddar, white Cheddar, or Monterey Jack (about 6 ounces)

Nonstick spray for the baking pan

1. Arrange the rack in the center of the oven and preheat the oven to 400°F. Place the sweet potatoes on a baking sheet and roast until soft, about 1 hour 15 minutes. Cool on a wire rack. Reduce the oven temperature to 350°F.

2. Roast the peppers by holding them with tongs or a long-handled fork over a gas burner on high; roast until charred, about 3 minutes for each pepper, turning them as their sides blacken. (Alternatively, roast them on a baking sheet 5 inches from a preheated broiler, turning them as they char, about 4 minutes total roasting time.) Place the blackened peppers in a paper bag or in a medium bowl tightly sealed with plastic wrap. Set aside for 15 minutes.

3. Toast the pepitas in a large skillet set over medium-low heat, about 4 minutes. Shake the skillet to keep the seeds from burning; they're done when they start to pop. Set aside.

4. When the potatoes are cool, peel them, then place them in a large bowl and mash with a potato masher or two forks. Do not beat. When the charred peppers are cool, peel them; cut the tops off, and gently seed and core them; set aside. Spray a 9 × 13-inch baking pan with nonstick spray.

5. Melt the butter in a large skillet set over medium-high heat. Add the onion and celery; sauté until soft and fragrant, about 4 minutes, stirring often. Stir these vegetables into the mashed sweet potatoes with a wooden spoon. Also stir in the toasted pepitas, brown sugar, chili powder, salt, and pepper.

6. Divide this mixture among the roasted pepper shells, about ¾ cup in each. If the peppers are firm enough to stand, place them in the prepared baking pan; otherwise, they can be laid on their sides, the filling spilling out slightly, like a cornucopia. Top with 2 tablespoons grated cheese, either sprinkled over the filling or over the pepper on its side.

7. Bake for 20 minutes, or until the cheese is bubbly and brown. Cool on a wire rack for 5 minutes, then serve.

Stir any one of the following into the sweet potato mixture:
½ cup canned crushed pineapple ✦ ½ cup mini-marshmallows ✦ ¼ cup chopped dried apricots ✦ ¼ cup dried cherries ✦ ¼ cup raisins ✦ ¼ cup shredded unsweetened coconut ✦ 2 tablespoons minced jalapeño pepper ✦ 1 teaspoon ground cinnamon ✦ 1 teaspoon ground ginger ✦ ¼ teaspoon grated nutmeg

You can also stuff this filling into poblano peppers rather than bell peppers. Choose 12 large poblanos and roast them as you would the bell peppers. They must lie on their sides, so the cheese should be sprinkled directly on the pepper, rather than on the filling.

Sweet-and-Sour Slow-Cooked Brisket {MAKES 6 SERVINGS}

This slow-cooked brisket uses two kinds of potatoes: sweet potatoes for taste and shredded baking potatoes for texture. The latter melt during the long cooking, slowly thickening the sweet-and-sour sauce with their starch. Therefore, the dish calls for no added fat yet still has a rich, deep taste. To make it even leaner, buy a flat-cut brisket, sometimes called a "first cut," which has less fat than the thicker "point cut." Because of its lower fat content, a first-cut brisket can be tough when barbecued, but it becomes exquisitely tender in a slow-cooker. Serve this one-pot meal with steamed green beans or an assortment of pickled vegetables.

2 pounds baking potatoes, such as Russets, scrubbed

1 large onion, minced

2 garlic cloves, minced

One 4- to 5-pound flat-cut brisket, trimmed of all visible fat and cut in half or thirds to fit into the slow-cooker

One 15-ounce can tomato sauce

One 6-ounce can tomato paste

½ cup cider vinegar

⅓ cup maple syrup

¼ cup unsulphured molasses

1 tablespoon Worcestershire sauce

2 teaspoons dry mustard

1 teaspoon salt, or to taste

½ teaspoon freshly ground black pepper

4 dashes Tabasco sauce, or to taste

2 pounds medium sweet potatoes, such as Jewels or Red Garnets, scrubbed, peeled, and cut into 1-inch-thick rounds

1. Peel the baking potatoes and finely shred them, using either the large holes of a box grater or a food processor fitted with the shredding blade. Place the shredded potatoes in the bottom of a 5-quart (or larger) slow-cooker; add the onion and garlic and toss to combine. Nestle the meat into this mixture.

2. In a large bowl, whisk together the tomato sauce, tomato paste, vinegar, syrup, molasses, Worcestershire sauce, dry mustard, salt, pepper, and Tabasco until smooth. Pour over the meat, making sure some of the sauce gets under it and mixes with the potatoes. Top with the sweet potato pieces.

3. Cover the slow-cooker and cook on high for 5 hours, or on low for 9 hours. Transfer the brisket to a cutting board and slice into ½-inch strips against the grain with the knife turned 45 degrees to the cutting surface. Return the meat to the slow-cooker and cook on high for 2 more hours, or until the meat is fork-tender. Serve immediately.

Extra Hot Sweet-and-Sour Brisket Add 2 teaspoons crushed red pepper flakes with the tomato sauce.

Honey Brisket Substitute ⅓ cup honey for the maple syrup.

Rum Brisket Add 3 tablespoons dark rum with the tomato sauce.

Spiced Brisket Add 1 teaspoon ground cinnamon, ½ teaspoon grated nutmeg, and ¼ teaspoon ground cloves with the tomato sauce.

Sweet-and-Sour Brisket with Cabbage Reduce the baking potatoes to 1 pound. Toss 1 pound shredded cabbage with the remaining shredded potatoes.

Sweet-and-Sour Brisket with Dried Fruits Add ½ cup raisins and ½ cup dried cherries to the tomato sauce, along with 1 extra tablespoon cider vinegar.

Sweet Potato Chili {MAKES 6 SERVINGS}

Ground buffalo now regularly shows up in supermarkets across the country. No longer just a gourmet's delight, it's a flavorful, low-fat alternative to beef. It balances this hearty chili, sweetened by sweet potatoes. To further enhance the flavors, use a dark beer such as Bass or even Guinness.

3 tablespoons canola or other vegetable oil

1 large onion, chopped

1 large green bell pepper, cored, seeded, and chopped

2 garlic cloves, minced

1½ pounds ground buffalo or ground sirloin

¼ cup chili powder

One 12-ounce bottle dark beer

2 pounds sweet potatoes, such as Jewels or Red Garnets, scrubbed

One 28-ounce can diced tomatoes, or whole tomatoes, diced, their juice reserved

One 4-ounce can chopped green chiles (hot, medium, or mild)

½ teaspoon salt, or to taste

½ teaspoon freshly ground black pepper

4 dashes Tabasco sauce, or to taste

1. Heat a large saucepan or pot over medium heat. Swirl in the oil, then add the onion and bell pepper. Cook until soft and fragrant, about 3 minutes, stirring often. Add the garlic, cook for 30 seconds, then stir in the ground buffalo. Cook just until it loses its raw color, stirring constantly, about a minute. Add the chili powder and cook for 30 seconds. Pour in the beer and let the mixture come to a simmer. Cook, uncovered, for 5 minutes, until the tomatoes begin to break down.

2. Meanwhile, peel the sweet potatoes and cut them into ½-inch pieces. Stir these pieces into the pot, along with the tomatoes (with their juice), green chiles, salt, pepper, and Tabasco sauce. Reduce the heat to low and simmer, uncovered, for 30 minutes, stirring occasionally.

3. Cover the pan and simmer another 30 minutes, stirring once or twice. Season with salt, if desired, and serve immediately.

Aromatic Sweet Potato Buffalo Chili Stir 1 teaspoon ground cinnamon, 1 teaspoon ground ginger, ¼ teaspoon grated nutmeg, and a pinch of ground cloves into the chili with the chili powder.

Sweet Potato Buffalo Chili and Beans Stir one 15-ounce can black beans, drained and rinsed, into the chili during its last 30 minutes of cooking.

Sweet Potato Turkey Chili Substitute ground turkey for the buffalo.

Szechwan Potatoes in Vinegar Sauce {MAKES 4 SERVINGS}

Szechwan cooks have long prepared this simple dish of potatoes in a sweet-and-sour sauce. What's unusual about this dish is that the potatoes are underdone by Western standards—crunchy and earthy, the preferred taste among Chinese cooks. To that end, use only fresh potatoes with no green spots. This dish would most likely be served over steamed mustard greens or alongside steamed bok choy.

1 ½ pounds yellow-fleshed potatoes, preferably Yukon Golds or Ozettes, scrubbed

3 tablespoons peanut or other vegetable oil

½ pound ground pork

4 scallions, green parts only, finely shredded

3 tablespoons minced fresh ginger

2 garlic cloves, minced

½ teaspoon crushed red pepper flakes, or to taste

3 tablespoons rice wine vinegar or white wine vinegar

1 ½ tablespoons soy sauce

1. Peel the potatoes, then finely shred them lengthwise, using the large holes of a box grater. Grate the potato slowly along its length to create the longest threads possible—don't use short jerky movements along the potato's short side. (Alternatively, you can use a food processor fitted with a shredding blade or a mandoline fitted with a shoestring blade, but the shredded potatoes will be shorter or thinner than are customarily used in this dish.)

2. Place the shredded potatoes in a colander and rinse two or three times to wash off excess starch. Squeeze the potatoes dry in the palms of your hands in batches over the sink, then set aside in a colander to drain for 5 minutes.

3. Heat a large nonstick wok or sauté pan over medium-high heat. Swirl in the oil, then add the pork and stir-fry for 1 minute. Add the scallions, ginger, garlic, and pepper flakes; stir-fry for 30 seconds, or until fragrant.

4. Stir in the potatoes; toss and cook for 1 minute. Add the vinegar and soy sauce; stir-fry for an additional 2 minutes, tossing and stirring constantly so the potatoes don't stick to the cooking surface. Serve immediately.

Aromatic Potatoes in Vinegar Sauce Add 2 teaspoons Szechwan peppercorns with the pork. Toss 3 tablespoons chopped cilantro into the dish just before serving.

Crab and Potatoes in Vinegar Sauce Omit the ground pork. Add ½ pound lump crabmeat, picked over for shell and cartilage, with the vinegar and soy sauce.

Potatoes and Beans in Vinegar Sauce Stir-fry ½ pound Chinese long beans, cut into ½-inch sections, with the pork.

Potatoes and Mushrooms in Vinegar Sauce Rehyrate 8 dried Chinese black mushrooms in hot water for 15 minutes. Drain, then thoroughly rinse for sand. Thinly slice the mushrooms and add them with the scallions.

Potatoes and Snow Peas in Vinegar Sauce Add 1 cup snow peas with the scallions.

Shrimp and Potatoes in Vinegar Sauce I Add ½ pound shrimp, peeled and deveined, with the pork.

Shrimp and Potatoes in Vinegar Sauce II Omit the pork. Stir-fry 1 pound shrimp, peeled, deveined, and coarsely chopped, in the oil before adding the other ingredients.

Tangy Potatoes in Vinegar Sauce Omit the red pepper flakes and soy sauce. Stir 2 tablespoons Hoisin sauce into the dish with the vinegar.

Vegetarian Potatoes in Vinegar Sauce Omit the pork. Stir-fry 8 ounces firm tofu, drained and cut into ½-inch cubes, in the oil until golden, about 3 minutes. Add 1 tablespoon additional oil if necessary.

Tapas

This recipe is actually a collection of four small tapas recipes. Together, they would make an excellent meal on the patio in the summer, or around the hearth in winter. Tapas are a Spanish tradition: little plates of food, served at the bar along with a glass of sherry. If you want to make all four of these dishes, boil two pounds red-skinned potatoes, peeled and diced, in a large pot of salted water for seven minutes, then use half a pound for each dish.

Potatoes and Calamari

½ pound red-skinned potatoes, scrubbed, peeled, and cut into ½-inch dice
2 tablespoons olive oil
1 large squid, or 3 small squid (about ½ pound), cleaned, cut into ¼-inch-thick
   rings (if desired, have your fishmonger clean the squid)
2 garlic cloves, minced
2 teaspoons sherry or white wine vinegar
½ teaspoon crushed red pepper flakes
½ teaspoon salt

1. Bring a medium pot of salted water to a boil. Add the potatoes and cook until tender when pierced with a fork, about 7 minutes. Drain and cool slightly.

2. Heat a large skillet (preferably nonstick) over medium-high heat. Swirl in the oil, then add the potatoes. Sauté until brown and crispy, about 6 minutes, stirring once or twice. Add the squid rings; cook until firm, about a minute. Stir in the garlic, vinegar, red pepper flakes, and salt. Cook for another 20 seconds, toss everything to coat, and serve immediately or at room temperature. (This dish is also quite tasty cold, after it's sat for a day, covered, in the refrigerator.)

Potatoes and Cheese

½ pound red-skinned potatoes, scrubbed, peeled, and cut into ½-inch dice

½ cup grated Manchego or other Spanish sheep's milk cheese (about 2 ounces)

¼ cup pitted oil-cured black olives, sliced (not water-packed)

2 tablespoons extra virgin olive oil

½ teaspoon salt

½ teaspoon freshly ground black pepper

1. Boil and drain the diced potatoes as in the first recipe.

2. Place the potatoes in a large bowl, along with the cheese, olives, olive oil, salt, and pepper. Toss to coat and serve. (This dish may be made up to two days ahead of time. Cover and refrigerate, but let come back to room temperature before serving.)

Potatoes and Chorizo

½ pound red-skinned potatoes, scrubbed, peeled, and cut into ½-inch dice

½ pound dried Spanish chorizo, cut in half lengthwise, then into ¼-inch-thick half-moons

2 garlic cloves, minced

2 tablespoons chopped fresh parsley

½ teaspoon salt

1. Boil and drain the diced potatoes as in the first recipe.

2. Heat a medium skillet (preferably nonstick) over medium heat. Add the chorizo and cook until it gives off its grease, about 3 minutes. Add the potatoes to the skillet along with the garlic and parsley. Cook until the potatoes crisp, about 5 minutes, stirring once or twice. Season with salt. Serve immediately or at room temperature.

Potatoes and Peppers

½ pound red-skinned potatoes, scrubbed, peeled, and cut into ½-inch dice

2 jarred pimientos, drained and cut into thin strips

2 tablespoons extra virgin olive oil

2 teaspoons chopped fresh oregano

½ teaspoon salt

½ teaspoon freshly ground black pepper

¼ teaspoon ground cayenne pepper

1. Boil and drain the diced potatoes as in the first recipe.

2. Place the potatoes in a large bowl along with the pimientos, olive oil, oregano, salt, pepper, and cayenne. Toss to coat and serve. (This dish may be made up to two days ahead of time. Cover and refrigerate, but let come back to room temperature before serving.)

Thai Curried Red Lentil Soup

{MAKES 4 SERVINGS}

In western Thailand, the indigenous flavors of Thai cooking blend with Indian influences that have come up via the trade routes over the mountains. This soup is a product of these culinary crossroads. The secret to the taste of this soup is Thai red curry paste, a fiery mélange of red chiles, garlic, and spices. If you have trouble finding it, check the Source Guide (page 251).

3 tablespoons canola or other vegetable oil

1 large onion, finely chopped

2 garlic cloves, minced

1 tablespoon minced fresh ginger

2 teaspoons Thai red curry paste

1 cup red lentils

4 cups (1 quart) vegetable or chicken stock, or more

1 bay leaf

1 pound red-skinned potatoes, such as Ruby Crescents or Red Blisses, scrubbed

1 teaspoon salt, or to taste

Yogurt (regular, low-fat, or fat-free), for garnish

Chopped cilantro, for garnish

1. Heat a large saucepan over medium heat. Swirl in the oil, then add the onion and cook until soft and fragrant, about 3 minutes, stirring frequently. Stir in the garlic, ginger, and curry paste; cook until fragrant, about 30 seconds, stirring constantly. Stir in the lentils, tossing to coat with the spices; then stir in the stock and bay leaf. Bring to a simmer.

2. Meanwhile, cut the potatoes into ½-inch dice. Once the soup is simmering, add them to the broth. Cover, reduce the heat to low, and simmer until the potatoes are soft when pierced with a fork, about 30 minutes, stirring occasionally. If the soup becomes too thick, thin it with more stock in ¼-cup increments. Discard the bay leaf; season with salt to taste. Serve immediately, passing the yogurt and cilantro alongside as garnishes. (You may keep this soup, covered, in the refrigerator for up to four days; thin it out with additional stock before reheating.)

Coconut Curried Red Lentil Soup Stir ½ cup unsweetened coconut milk into the dish just before serving.

Nutty Red Lentil Soup Stir 1 cup chopped almonds and ½ cup raisins into the soup with the potatoes.

Red Lentil and Apple Soup Peel, core, and roughly chop 2 Granny Smith apples. Stir them into the soup with the potatoes.

Red Lentil Soup with a Peanut Satay Sauce Stir 2 tablespoons bottled satay sauce and ¼ cup unsalted roasted peanuts into the dish just before serving.

Shrimp and Red Lentil Soup Stir ½ pound medium shrimp (about 35 per pound), peeled and deveined, into the dish once the lentils are tender. Cook 3 more minutes, then serve.

Thai Curried Yellow Lentil Soup Substitute yellow Thai curry paste (much hotter) for the red; substitute yellow lentils (not yellow split peas) for the red lentils. Substitute yellow-fleshed potatoes for the red-skinned ones.

Tofu Soup

This is a light Japanese broth soup, a little sweet, but packed with treasures. Buy extra firm tofu, so it doesn't break down in the broth. You might also try a fat-free tofu, now showing up in health food and gourmet stores.

Cellophane noodles—or bean thread noodles, mung bean noodles, glass noodles or *fen si* in Chinese—are thread-like noodles made from ground mung beans. They are available dried in Asian markets and usually in the Asian section of most grocery stores. Rehydrate dried cellophane noodles by covering them with hot water in a large bowl. Let them stand for ten minutes, or until they turn translucent, then drain.

4 ounces cellophane noodles

4 cups (1 quart) hot water

1 pound red-skinned potatoes, such as Ruby Crescent fingerlings, French Fingerlings, or All Reds, scrubbed

¼ pound snow peas

8 cups (2 quarts) vegetable stock or mushroom stock

5 tablespoons mirin

1 tablespoon soy sauce (regular or low-sodium)

1 pound extra firm tofu, cut into 1-inch pieces

¼ pound shiitake mushrooms, stemmed, cleaned, the caps thinly sliced

6 scallions, thinly sliced

1. Place the cellophane noodles in a large bowl; pour the hot water over them. Set aside to soak until soft and translucent, about 10 minutes. Drain, then set aside on a plate, covered with a damp towel or moistened paper towels.

2. Bring a medium pot of salted water to a boil. Meanwhile, peel the potatoes and cut them into 1-inch pieces. Add them to the boiling water and cook until tender when pierced with a fork, about 9 minutes. Add the snow peas, blanch for an additional 30 seconds, then drain all.

3. Combine the stock, mirin, and soy sauce in a large pot; bring the mixture to a slow simmer over medium heat. Fluff the cellophane noodles so they aren't stuck in one clump, then stir them into the broth, along with the cooked potatoes, blanched snow peas, tofu, mushrooms, and scallions.

4. Return to a slow simmer, adjusting the heat so the liquid is not at a boil but just the barest bubble. Cook for 5 minutes without stirring so that the potatoes don't cloud the broth. Serve immediately.

Ladle the soup over one or two of the following placed decoratively in the bowls: bean sprouts ✦ carrots, shredded ✦ celery, thinly sliced ✦ cocktail shrimp, pre-cooked ✦ cucumbers, thinly sliced ✦ daikon radish, thinly shredded ✦ garlic sprouts ✦ lump crabmeat, picked over for shell and cartilage ✦ radish sprouts ✦ scallops, raw, thinly sliced (the heat of the broth will cook them) ✦ small spinach leaves, washed

{MAKES 6 SERVINGS} # Tsimmes

This sweet potato dish is a Jewish tradition on Rosh Hashanah, the high holiday of the New Year, celebrated around mid-September. Quite sweet, tsimmes is said to symbolize the hope for a sweet year ahead. It's a meal in itself, a meat-and-potato lover's dream come true.

1 pound first-cut beef brisket

1½ pounds sweet potatoes, such as Jewels or Red Garnets, scrubbed

1 pound carrots

1 pound parsnips

½ cup pitted prunes

3 cups beef or chicken stock

¼ cup honey

1 teaspoon salt, or to taste

½ teaspoon ground cinnamon

½ teaspoon freshly ground black pepper

Nonstick spray for the baking dish

1. Bring a large pot of salted water to a boil. Add the brisket and boil for 30 minutes.

2. Meanwhile, peel the sweet potatoes and cut them into 1-inch pieces; place in a large bowl. Peel the carrots and parsnips and cut them into 1-inch rounds; combine in the bowl with the sweet potato pieces. Position the rack in the center of the oven and preheat the oven to 325°F. Spray a 9 × 13-inch baking pan with nonstick spray and set it aside.

3. Drain the brisket and cool slightly, then cut against the grain into ½-inch chunks. Mix these pieces with the vegetables; stir in the prunes.

4. In a small bowl, whisk 2½ cups of the stock, the honey, salt, cinnamon, and pepper together until well combined. Pour this sauce over the meat and vegetable mixture. Toss to coat, then pour into the prepared baking dish, spreading the mixture evenly throughout. Cover with foil and bake for 2 hours 30 minutes.

5. Remove the foil and stir in the remaining ½ cup stock. Bake for 30 minutes, or until the meat is fork-tender. Cool in the baking pan on a wire rack for 5 minutes, then serve.

Chicken Tsimmes Substitute 1 pound boneless, skinless chicken breasts, cut into 1-inch pieces, for the beef. Do not boil the chicken first; simply roast the vegetables and prunes for 1 hour, then stir in the chicken pieces and ½ cup stock. Cover and cook for 1 additional hour, then serve.

New England Tsimmes Add 1 cup dried cranberries and ½ cup chopped walnuts to the meat and vegetable mixture.

Sausage Tsimmes Substitute 1 pound veal or chicken sausage, cut into 1-inch chunks, for the beef. Boil for 15 minutes.

Turkey Tsimmes Substitute 1 pound boneless, skinless turkey breast, cut into 1-inch pieces, for the beef. Do not boil the turkey first. Add it to the pan along with ½ cup stock after the vegetables have roasted for 1 hour. Cover and cook for 1 additional hour, then serve.

{makes 6 servings} # Turkey Pot Pie

With puff pastry dough available in the freezer section of your supermarket, homemade turkey pot pies can be ready in no time. Let the dough thaw in its package in the refrigerator for twenty-four hours before using.

2 pounds white potatoes, such as Irish Cobblers, Kennebecs, or Long Whites, scrubbed

5 tablespoons unsalted butter, at room temperature

1 medium onion, chopped

2 celery stalks, thinly sliced

1 pound cremini or button mushrooms, cleaned and thinly sliced

1 pound boneless turkey breast or turkey cutlets, cut into 1-inch chunks

2 teaspoons salt, or to taste

1/2 teaspoon freshly ground black pepper

2 tablespoons minced fresh sage

2 tablespoons fresh thyme

2 tablespoons brandy

1/4 cup all-purpose flour, plus additional for the work surface

3 cups chicken stock

1/2 cup heavy cream

One 14-ounce package frozen puff pastry, thawed

1. Position the rack in the center of the oven and then preheat the oven to 350°F.

2. Bring a medium pot of salted water to a boil. Meanwhile, peel the potatoes and cut them into 1-inch pieces. Add them to the boiling water; cook until still firm when pierced with a fork, about 7 minutes. Drain and cool slightly.

3. In a large skillet or sauté pan, melt 2 tablespoons of the butter over medium heat. Add the onion and celery; cook until soft and fragrant, about 4 minutes, stirring often. Add the mushrooms and cook until they release their liquid, about 3 minutes, stirring occasionally. Stir in the turkey meat, salt, and pepper; cook just until the turkey loses its raw, pink color. Then stir in the sage and thyme and cook for 30 seconds. Stir in the cooked potatoes and the brandy. (The pan may flame—if it does, cover it and take it off the heat for 1 minute.) Toss so everything is well combined, then set aside while you make the béchamel.

4. In a medium skillet, melt the remaining 3 tablespoons butter over medium heat. Whisk in the flour and cook for 30 seconds, whisking constantly—do not brown the flour. Continue whisking as you drizzle in the stock in a slow, steady stream, then whisk in the cream all at once. Continue whisking until the mixture thickens, about a minute. Pour this béchamel over the potato mixture, toss to distribute evenly, and pour into a 9 × 13-inch baking dish or a 12-cup casserole.

5. Unwrap the puff pastry, place it on a lightly floured work surface, and lightly roll it an extra inch in all directions, just to loosen the dough and make it fit the pan. Roll gently—do not bear down or the dough will not rise. Place the puff pastry sheet over the baking dish, crimping its edges down and together. You want it large enough to overlap the edges of the baking dish slightly, or at least bunch up against the inside edge.

6. Bake for 45 minutes, or until the pastry topping is puffed and brown. Let stand for 10 minutes, then serve.

Substitute any one of the following for the turkey:
1 pound ground beef or beef tenderloin, cut into 1-inch cubes ✦ 1 pound boneless, skinless chicken breasts, or chicken cutlets, cut into 1-inch cubes ✦ 1 pound pork tenderloin, cut into 1-inch pieces ✦ 1 pound large shrimp (15 to 25 per pound), peeled and deveined

You can also substitute equivalent amounts of sweet potatoes or purple potatoes for the white potatoes.

Twice-Baked Potatoes

Russet potatoes work best here, because their flesh is dry enough to become crisp during the first baking, yet starchy enough to withstand the second baking, once the potatoes are filled.

4 large baking potatoes, preferably Russets, scrubbed

1 teaspoon canola or other vegetable oil

4 strips bacon

1 cup water

12 thin asparagus spears, trimmed

½ cup heavy cream

2 tablespoons unsalted butter, at room temperature

1 teaspoon sweet paprika

1 teaspoon onion powder

½ teaspoon garlic powder

½ teaspoon salt

½ teaspoon freshly ground black pepper

½ cup grated Cheddar (about 2 ounces)

1 tablespoon plus 1 teaspoon chopped fresh chives

1. Position the rack in the center of the oven and preheat the oven to 350°F. Place the potatoes in the center of the rack and bake until soft, about 1 hour 15 minutes. Remove to a wire rack and cool. Raise the oven temperature to 375°F.

2. Heat a large skillet (preferably nonstick) over medium heat. Swirl in the oil, then add the bacon and fry until brown and crisp, turning once, about 3 minutes per side. Drain the bacon on a plate lined with paper towels; crumble and set aside.

3. Discard any rendered fat in the skillet; wash the skillet and return to high heat. Add the water, bring it to a boil, then add the asparagus. Cover and cook until the spears are tender but still crisp, about 3 minutes. Drain

POTATO RECIPES, A TO Z ✦ 235

and run cold water over the spears to stop them from cooking. Cut 4 spears into ½-inch pieces; set them aside. Reserve the remaining 8 spears whole.

4. When the potatoes are cool enough to handle, slice the top third off each potato lengthwise. Use a small spoon to scoop out the insides of the larger sections of each potato into a large bowl, leaving ⅛ inch of flesh against the skin so that it will not collapse when stuffed and re-baked. Scoop the insides of the cut-off top sections into the bowl as well. Discard the top skins.

5. Beat the cream and butter into the scooped-out potato flesh with an electric mixer at medium speed, about 2 minutes. (Alternatively, use a potato masher—press down gently but firmly into the potatoes as you mash them with the cream.) Add the paprika, onion powder, garlic powder, salt, and pepper; beat until creamy, about 2 minutes with a mixer or 4 minutes by hand. Gently fold in the crumbled bacon and cut-up asparagus spears, using a rubber spatula.

6. Place the four potato-skin shells in a 9 × 13-inch baking dish. Lay 2 whole asparagus spears in each shell the long way, so that the asparagus ends droop out the sides. Divide the mashed potato mixture among the four potato-skin shells, covering the asparagus and mounding the mixture with a spoon. Sprinkle each stuffed potato with 2 tablespoons Cheddar and 1 teaspoon chives. Bake for 15 minutes, or until the cheese is melted and the stuffing is heated through. Serve immediately.

Cheesy Twice-Baked Potatoes Add ½ cup crumbled Gorgonzola or other blue cheese (about 2 ounces) and ½ cup grated Asiago cheese (about 2 ounces) to the potato and cream mixture before baking.

Crab-Stuffed Twice-Baked Potatoes Stir ½ pound lump crabmeat, picked over for shell and cartilage, into the potato stuffing mixture.

Green Bean–Stuffed Twice-Baked Potatoes Omit the asparagus. Blanch ½ pound green beans, then chop 6 beans for the filling. Divide the remaining beans among the potato skins, laying them inside as you would the asparagus.

Shrimp-Stuffed Twice-Baked Potatoes Omit the bacon. Coarsely chop ½ pound shrimp and sauté it in the oil in a large skillet set over medium heat, for about 2 minutes, until pink and firm. Roughly chop the shrimp and fold into the potato stuffing mixture.

Twice-Baked Yams Omit the russets. Use 4 large, thick Garnet Yams instead.

Vegetarian Twice-Baked Potatoes Omit the bacon and the oil. Sauté ½ pound button or cremini mushrooms, cleaned and sliced, in 2 tablespoons unsalted butter in a large skillet set over medium heat until they soften and give off their liquid, and the liquid evaporates, about 4 minutes, stirring frequently. Add the sautéed mushrooms along with one 10-ounce package mixed frozen vegetables, thawed, to the mashed potato mixture.

Vegetarian Chili {MAKES 8 SERVINGS}

This chunky chili is best served the minute it's made—as the potatoes sit, they release their starch, thickening the chili considerably. (For a smoother chili, see Sweet Potato Chili, page 220.) For a novel presentation, serve it in small, round, hollowed-out loaves of bread.

2 tablespoons canola or other vegetable oil

1 large onion, chopped

2 celery stalks, chopped

1 medium green bell pepper, cored, seeded, and diced

2 garlic cloves, minced

¼ cup chili powder

One 12-ounce bottle beer, preferably a Hefeweise or Belgian White beer

One 28-ounce can diced tomatoes, or whole tomatoes, diced, their juice reserved

One 15-ounce can kidney beans, drained and rinsed

1 pound red-skinned potatoes, such as All Reds, French Fingerlings, or Ruby
   Crescent fingerlings, scrubbed

1 teaspoon salt

½ teaspoon freshly ground black pepper

4 dashes Tabasco sauce, or to taste

1. Heat a large saucepan or pot over medium heat. Swirl in the oil, then add the onion and celery. Cook until soft and fragrant, about 4 minutes, stirring often. Add the bell pepper and cook for 1 minute, stirring constantly. Then add the garlic and chili powder; cook for 30 seconds.

2. Raise the heat to medium-high; stir in the beer and tomatoes (along with their juice). Scrape up any browned bits on the bottom of the pan, then stir in the beans. Bring to a simmer and cook, uncovered, for 5 minutes.

3. Meanwhile, peel the potatoes and cut them into ½-inch pieces. Add them to the stew and reduce the heat to low. Simmer, partially covered, until the potatoes are tender when pierced with a fork, about 30 minutes; stir the chili often to avoid sticking. Season with salt, pepper, and Tabasco sauce. Serve immediately or store tightly covered in the refrigerator for up to three days.

Add any of these things to the chili along with the potatoes together with 1½ cups vegetable stock. Increase the chili powder by 1 tablespoon.
one 15-ounce can black beans, drained and rinsed ✦ one 15-ounce can chickpeas, drained and rinsed ✦ one 15-ounce can cream-style corn ✦ one 15-ounce can pinto beans, drained and rinsed ✦ one 10-ounce package frozen corn, thawed ✦ one 10-ounce package frozen peas, thawed

You can also top this chili with:
chopped cilantro ✦ chopped pickles ✦ crushed tortilla chips ✦ diced tomatoes ✦ minced red onions ✦ pickled jalapeños ✦ shredded carrots ✦ shredded Cheddar, Colby, or Monterey Jack ✦ shredded jicama ✦ sliced jalapeño peppers ✦ sour cream ✦ toasted pecans ✦ toasted pepitas ✦ yogurt

Venetian Pasta e Patate {MAKES 4 SERVINGS}

Whenever you buy clams, ask to smell them first to make sure they're fresh. They should smell clean and briny—not like the tidal flats at low tide. Rinse the clams in cold water, scrub off any grit, then store them for no more than five hours in the refrigerator, surrounded and covered very loosely by damp paper towels.

1½ pounds round white potatoes, such as Creamers or Maris Pipers, scrubbed

3 tablespoons olive oil

10 garlic cloves, minced

1 cup dry vermouth or white wine, or more as necessary

1 teaspoon chopped fresh oregano

¾ teaspoon crushed red pepper flakes

½ teaspoon salt

½ teaspoon freshly ground black pepper

2 pounds small clams, such as littlenecks or Pismos

1 pound dry linguine, cooked according to package directions, drained, and rinsed

2 tablespoons unsalted butter

2 tablespoons chopped fresh parsley

1. Cut the potatoes into ½-inch pieces. Place them in a large bowl, cover with cool water, and let stand for 10 minutes. Drain and set aside.

2. Heat a large saucepan or sauté pan over medium heat. Swirl in the oil, then add the garlic and cook until fragrant, about a minute, stirring constantly. Add the potatoes; cook just until the potatoes begin to soften, about 4 minutes, stirring often. Stir in ½ cup of the vermouth, cover, and simmer for 10 minutes, stirring occasionally to make sure the potatoes don't stick to the bottom of the pan. If the liquid evaporates too quickly, add more vermouth in 2-tablespoon increments.

3. Once the potatoes begin to soften, gently stir in another ½ cup vermouth, then add the oregano, red pepper flakes, salt, and pepper. Bring the mixture to a simmer and add the clams, discarding any that will not close when tapped. Cover the pan, reduce the heat to medium-low, and simmer until the clams open, about 6 minutes.

4. Discard any clams that do not open. To avoid mashing the potatoes, gently stir in the cooked linguine, then top with the butter and parsley. Serve immediately.

Hearty Pasta e Patate Reduce the vermouth to ½ cup and add it only to simmer the potatoes. Add ½ cup beer before the spices.

Pasta e Patate with Crab Substitute 1 pound lump crabmeat, picked over for shells and cartilage, for the clams.

Pasta e Patate with Mussels Substitute 2 pounds mussels, scrubbed and debearded, for the clams.

Pasta e Patate with Pancetta Before adding the garlic, fry ½ pound pancetta, finely diced, in the olive oil. Decrease the salt to taste.

Pasta e Patate with Shrimp Substitute 1 pound medium shrimp (about 35 per pound), peeled and deveined, for the clams. Reduce the shrimp's cooking time to 3 minutes, or until they are firm and pink.

Vindaloo {MAKES 4 SERVINGS}

Although this dish is usually associated with India, vindaloo is actually of colonial extraction. Its name means "wine and garlic" in Portuguese; it was a homespun dish served in the kitchens of that nation's colonies on India's western flank. But the Indians did the colonialists one better by turning this dish into a fiery stew. This vindaloo can be easily doubled—or even tripled—if you have a pot big enough.

3 tablespoons canola or other vegetable oil

1 large onion, thinly sliced

4 garlic cloves, minced

½ teaspoon crushed red pepper flakes

1 teaspoon ground coriander

1 teaspoon turmeric

1 teaspoon salt, or to taste

1 teaspoon freshly ground black pepper

½ teaspoon ground cumin

½ teaspoon ground cinnamon

½ teaspoon ground ginger

¼ teaspoon ground cardamom

¼ teaspoon ground cloves

2 tablespoons white wine vinegar

One 28-ounce can diced tomatoes, or whole tomatoes, diced, their juice reserved

1½ pounds small red-skinned potatoes, preferably Red Blisses, scrubbed and quartered

One 10-ounce package frozen spinach, thawed and squeezed of any excess moisture

1. Heat a large pot over medium heat. Swirl in the oil, then add the onion and cook until soft and fragrant, about 3 minutes, stirring often. Add the garlic; cook for 30 seconds. Stir in the red pepper flakes, coriander, turmeric, salt, pepper, cumin, cinnamon, ginger, cardamom, cloves, and vinegar; cook for 10 seconds, just until the spices become fragrant, stirring constantly. (Be careful as the cayenne oil volatilizes—the vapors can burn your eyes.)

2. Add the tomatoes (and their juice) and bring the mixture to a simmer. Stir in the potatoes and reduce the heat to low. Cover and cook for 15 minutes, stirring occasionally.

3. Stir in the spinach and cook for another 20 minutes, uncovered, stirring often but gently—be careful not to mash the potatoes. Serve immediately.

Omit the spinach and add one of any the following to the stew:
2 cups shredded chicory or dandelion greens (about 1 large bunch, washed) ✦ 2 cups stemmed and shredded mustard or collard greens (about 1 large bunch, washed) ✦ 2 cups stemmed and shredded Swiss chard (about 1 large bunch, washed) ✦ 2 cups stemmed watercress (about 2 bunches) ✦ one 10-ounce package frozen peas, thawed ✦ one 10-ounce package frozen mixed vegetables, thawed ✦ 2 medium chayotes, cut into 1-inch cubes ✦ 2 medium zucchinis, cut into 1-inch-thick rings ✦ 2 large green bell peppers, cored, seeded, and diced

Whole Roasted Snapper

{MAKES 4 SERVINGS}

This light, flavorful dish makes a glorious presentation. The thin potato slices are baked first, so they turn golden brown and crispy, then the whole fish is laid on top. To create potato slices this thin, you'll need either a mandoline or a one-millimeter blade for your food processor—or excellent knife technique. Have your fishmonger clean and scale the fish, but leave it whole for the best presentation.

¼ cup fresh thyme
¼ cup chopped fresh parsley
¾ cup olive oil
3 pounds baking potatoes, preferably Russets, scrubbed
6 garlic cloves, minced
2 teaspoons salt
1½ teaspoons freshly ground black pepper
One 4-pound whole red snapper, cleaned and scaled
4 sprigs fresh rosemary
1 cup small, pitted, oil-cured black olives (not water-packed)

1. Position the rack in the bottom third of the oven and preheat the oven to 400°F. In a small bowl, mix the thyme and parsley until well combined. Oil a 12-cup roasting pan (preferably an oval pan) or a baking dish with 2 tablespoons of the olive oil.

2. Peel the potatoes and thinly slice them, using either a mandoline adjusted to the thinnest slicing position or a food processor fitted with a 1-millimeter slicing blade. (Alternatively, you can slice the potatoes by hand—use a sharp chef's knife and make the thinnest cuts possible.)

3. Make an overlapping layer of these potato slices across the bottom of the roasting pan. Sprinkle the potatoes with 1 tablespoon of the herb mixture,

1½ teaspoons minced garlic, ¼ teaspoon of the salt, and ⅛ teaspoon of the pepper; then drizzle with 2 tablespoons of the olive oil. Repeat this process until all the potatoes are used, creating at least three layers, possibly four. (The number of layers will depend on the shape of the baking dish and how far you overlap the potatoes. Less overlap and the potatoes are crisper; more overlap and they're chewier.) The final layer should be only potatoes, no herbs or garlic, drizzled with 2 tablespoons of the olive oil. (Reserve the remaining oil, herbs, garlic, and spices for the fish.)

4. Bake for 40 minutes, or until the potatoes are golden and crispy. Cool on a wire rack for 5 minutes. Reduce the oven temperature to 350°F.

5. Meanwhile, rinse the fish and pat it dry. Rub its skin with the remaining olive oil; stuff its cavity with the remaining herbs, garlic, salt, and pepper, as well as the rosemary sprigs.

6. Sprinkle the olives over the baked potatoes. Place the prepared fish on top of the olives and potatoes. Bake for 45 minutes, or about 15 minutes per inch of the fish's thickness.

7. Transfer the fish to a serving platter with two spatulas (so that no bones fall into the potatoes as the fish is sliced). Gently slice the fish or pull off the meat using a fork. Scoop up the potatoes and olives to serve alongside.

Sprinkle other items around the fish before you bake it, including:
2 teaspoons minced lemon zest ✦ 2 teaspoons minced basil ✦ 12 cherry tomatoes ✦ 4 thinly sliced scallions

During the last 15 minutes of baking, sprinkle the following around the fish:
1 pound mussels, scrubbed and debearded (discard any that do not open after baking) ✦ 1 cup crumbled feta cheese ✦ 1 cup crumbled Gorgonzola or other blue cheese

Potato Recipes Listed by Type of Potato Used

If you come home with a specific potato in hand and want a recipe that uses it, here's a list to help.

Baking potatoes

Argentinean Empanadas ✦ Barbecued Pulled Pork with Potatoes ✦ Beef Stew with Duchess Potatoes ✦ Blintzes ✦ Caldo Verde ✦ Chicken and Dumplings ✦ Chili Fries ✦ Cod Cakes ✦ Coffee Cake ✦ Fish and Chips ✦ Knishes ✦ Lasagna ✦ Meat Loaf ✦ Moussaka ✦ Nikujaga ✦ Pierogi Pie ✦ Potato Skins ✦ Potato-Crusted Cod ✦ Potatoes Sarladaise ✦ Quiche ✦ Ravioli ✦ Reuben Rolls ✦ Scrapple ✦ Shepherd's Pie ✦ Shrimp Balls ✦ Skordalia on Grilled Shrimp ✦ Twice-Baked Potatoes ✦ Whole Roasted Snapper

Russet potatoes specifically

Gnocchi ✦ Noodles with Mushrooms

A combination of baking potatoes and other potatoes

Ajiaco ✦ Sweet-and-Sour Slow-Cooked Brisket

White potatoes

Aloo Mutar Gobi ✦ Bangers and Mash ✦ Borscht ✦ Bubble and Squeak ✦ Ceviche ✦ Coconut Curry Ragoût ✦ Irish Stew ✦ Red Cooking Pork ✦ Soufflé ✦ Spanish Omelet ✦ Turkey Pot Pie ✦ Venetian Pasta e Patate

Yellow-fleshed potatoes

Charlotte ✦ Curry ✦ Frittata ✦ Galette ✦ Gratin ✦ Latkes with a Quick Applesauce ✦ Leek Soup ✦ Manhattan Clam Chowder ✦ Norwegian Potato Salad ✦ Paprikash ✦ Pasta Salad with Roasted Red Pepper Pesto ✦ Rice, Potatoes, and Shrimp ✦ Roesti ✦ Southern Potatoes and Greens Casserole ✦ Spanish Potato Salad ✦ Split Pea Soup ✦ Steak Frites ✦ Steamed Mussels and Potatoes ✦ Szechwan Potatoes in Vinegar Sauce

Red-skinned potatoes

Clam Bake ✦ Corned Beef and Cabbage ✦ Focaccia ✦ German Potato Salad ✦ Gesmoorde Vis ✦ Masala Dosa ✦ New England Clam Chowder ✦ Pork and Potato Stir-Fry ✦ Pot Roast ✦ Provençal Stew ✦ Quesadillas ✦ Smoked Pork Chops with Sauerkraut and Potatoes ✦ Smoked Salmon Potato Salad ✦ Tapas ✦ Thai Curried Red Lentil Soup ✦ Tofu Soup ✦ Vegetarian Chili ✦ Vindaloo

Yellow-fleshed *and* red-skinned potatoes

Mushroom Stew ✦ Salade Niçoise

Yellow-fleshed *or* red-skinned potatoes

French Potato Salad ✦ Fried Potatoes with Shrimp and Garlic ✦ Fondue ✦ Raclette

Red-skinned potatoes and sweet potatoes

Hash ✦ Ma'afe

Purple potatoes

Enchiladas ✦ Purple Potato and Black Bean Soup ✦ Purple Potato Tamales ✦ Salpiçon

Sweet potatoes

Autumn Chestnut Rice ✦ Curried Mushroom Soup ✦ Hot Cakes ✦ Japanese Mushrooms with a Sweet Potato Infusion ✦ Stuffed Peppers ✦ Sweet Potato Chili ✦ Tsimmes

Source Guide

Boyajian
349 Lenox Street
Norwood, MA 02062
1-800-419-4677
www.boyajianinc.com
A wide range of flavored oils and vinegars, as well as the most fragrant peanut oil on the market. Although many of these products are available at supermarkets and gourmet stores, the collection is available on Boyajian's website.

Broadway Panhandler
477 Broome Street
New York, NY 10013
1-866-COOKWARE or 1-212-966-3434
www.broadwaypanhandler.com
Potato ricers and the Cook's Helper, a Japanese tool to make shoestring fries, as well as a complete set of kitchen tools, including graters and mandolines.

Kalustyan's
123 Lexington Avenue
New York, NY 10016
1-212-685-3451
www.kalustyans.com
An extensive assortment of herbs, spices, oils, nuts, and flavorings, specializing in Indian products. A great source for kaffir lime leaves.

Kam Man Food Products
200 Canal Street
New York, NY 10013
1-212-571-0330
New York's finest Asian grocery and cookware store. Canned and dried Chinese vegetables, as well as a comprehensive line of Asian oils, vinegars, sauces, and dried noodles.

Kitchen Market
218 Eighth Avenue
New York, NY 10011
1-888-408-4433
A great source for Spanish chorizo, as well as most Latin American and Mexican foods, including chiles and spices.

Nervous Nellie's Jams and Jellies
598 Sunshine Road
Deer Isle, ME 04627
1-800-777-6845
www.nervousnellies.com
The best hot tomato chutney we know, plus others, like wild Maine blueberry and rhubarb ginger.

Pacific Rim Gourmet
1-800-618-7575
www.pacificrim-gourmet.com
An online gourmet resource with a full range of ingredients and Asian kitchenware.

Sur La Table
Stores across the country
1-800-243-0852
www.surlatable.com
A complete line of cookware, including potato ricers, graters, mandolines, and the Cook's Helper.

ThaiGrocer
2961 N. Sheridan Rd.
Chicago, IL 60657
1-773-988-8424
www.thaigrocer.com
One of the most complete Thai grocers, offering exotic canned fruits and vegetables, sauces, condiments, chili pastes, noodles, oils, vinegars, and rice flour.

The Wok Shop
718 Grant Avenue
San Francisco, CA 94108
1-888-780-7171
www.wokshop.com
In the heart of San Francisco's Chinatown, a huge assortment of woks, bamboo steamers, cleavers, and other Asian cooking equipment. Nearly everything is available online.

Uwajimaya
519 6th Ave. South
Seattle, WA 98104
1-206-624-6248
www.uwajimaya.com
An enormous Asian grocery store and order center with three retail outlets in Washington state.

Ultimatecook
www.ultimatecook.com
Extra recipes and information on all the Ultimate Books, as well as a complete list of links to our favorite food mail-order sources.

Index

Swiss chard:
    and potatoes casserole, 204
    tamales, barbecued, 165
Szechwan:
    barbecued pulled pork, 34
    potatoes in vinegar sauce,
        222–23

tamales:
    chicken, 165
    mushroom, 165
    purple potato, 163–65
    Swiss chard, 165
    Thai purple corn, 165
tapas, 224–25
tartar sauce, for fish and
        chips, 77
Thai:
    curried lentil soup, 227–28
    purple corn tamales, 165
tofu:
    red cooking, 176
    soup, 229–30
    -yaga, 136
tomato(es):
    in chili fries, 54–55
    in curry, 70–71
    in gesmoorde vis, 93–94
    in Manhattan clam
        chowder, 120

paprikash, 143
in Provençal stew, 159–60
sauce, fresh, for gnocchi, 97
and smoked pork chops,
    198
in Spanish omelet, 205–6
in steamed mussels and
    potatoes, 214–15
sun-dried, and potato
    ravioli, 174
in sweet potato chili,
    220–21
in vegetarian chili, 238–39
in vindaloo, 242–43
tsimmes, 231–32
tuna steak, in salad niçoise,
    183–84
turkey:
    and dumplings, 53
    pot pie, 233–34
    sausage, split pea soup
        with, 211
    smoked, charlotte, 50
    smoked, Reuben rolls,
        178
    sweet potato chili with, 221
    tsimmes, 232
turnip, leek and potato soup
    with, 117
twice-baked potatoes, 235–37

veal:
    ground, in shepherd's pie,
        191
    in paprikash, 142–43
vegetables, see specific
    vegetables
vegetable soup, split pea and,
    211
vegetarian:
    caldo verde, 45
    chili, 238–39
    curry, 70–71
    ma'afe, 118–19
    masala dosa, 122–24
    moussaka, 130
    potato lasagna, 113
    shepherd's pie, 191
    Szechwan potatoes in
        vinegar sauce, 223
    twice-baked potatoes, 237
Venetian pasta e patate, 240–41
vindaloo, 242–43

whole roasted snapper,
    244–45
Wisconsin brats and mash, 32

yams, twice-baked, 237
yellow lentil soup, Thai
    curried, 228